AGAINST THE DEATH PENALTY

AGAINST
THE
DEATH
PENALTY

JUSTICE STEPHEN BREYER

Edited by John Bessler

BROOKINGS INSTITUTION PRESS

Washington, D.C.

The Brookings Institution is a private nonprofit organization devoted to research, education, and publication on important issues of domestic and foreign policy. Its principal purpose is to bring the highest quality independent research and analysis to bear on current and emerging policy problems. Interpretations or conclusions in Brookings publications should be understood to be solely those of the authors.

This book reprints Justice Stephen Breyer's dissent in *Glossip v. Gross,* 135 S. Ct. 2726 (2015), text taken from the public record. Justice Breyer does not receive any compensation or remuneration for this book. The Brookings Institution, which has been publishing Stephen Breyer's work since the 1970s (Stephen G. Breyer and Paul W. MacAvoy, *Energy Regulation by the Federal Power Commission,* 1974; Stephen Breyer, *Economic Reasoning and Judicial Review,* 2004), thanks *The Atlantic* for granting permission to reprint material contained in the appendices of *Glossip v. Gross.*

Library of Congress Cataloging-in-Publication Data
Names: Breyer, Stephen G., 1938– author. | Bessler, John D., editor, writer of introduction.
Title: Against the death penalty / Justice Stephen Breyer ; edited by John Bessler.
Description: Washington : Brookings Institution Press, 2016.
Identifiers: LCCN 2016017499 (print) | LCCN 2016017695 (ebook) | ISBN 9780815728894 (hardback) | ISBN 9780815740568 (paperback) | ISBN 9780815728900 (ebook)
Subjects: LCSH: Capital punishment—United States. | BISAC: POLITICAL SCIENCE / Government / Judicial Branch. | POLITICAL SCIENCE / Constitutions. | POLITICAL SCIENCE / Political Freedom & Security / Human Rights. | POLITICAL SCIENCE / Political Process / General.
Classification: LCC KF9227.C2 B74 2016 (print) | LCC KF9227.C2 (ebook) | DDC 345.73/0773—dc23
LC record available at https://lccn.loc.gov/2016017499

9 8 7 6 5 4 3 2 1

Typeset in Sabon
Composition by Westchester Publishing Services

CONTENTS

AGAINST THE DEATH PENALTY

INTRODUCTION

John Bessler

AT THE NATION'S HIGHEST COURT

On April 29, 2015, the Supreme Court of the United States heard oral arguments in *Glossip v. Gross*.[1] The named petitioner, Richard Glossip, had been convicted of first-degree murder for asking another man, Justin Sneed, to kill their mutual boss, Barry Van Treese. On January 7, 1997, Van Treese's body was discovered in Room 102 of Oklahoma City's Best Budget Inn, which Van Treese owned. Glossip had worked as the manager of the seedy motel, and Sneed, age nineteen, lived there rent-free in exchange for doing maintenance work. Van Treese had died of blood loss and blunt force trauma to his head, with Sneed getting a black eye during the course of the killing. Sneed later pled guilty to the murder, admitting that he had hit Van Treese with a baseball bat "ten or fifteen times." At Glossip's first trial in 1998, the jury found that Van Treese was killed for remuneration, and Glossip was convicted and sentenced to death. Sneed—an eighth-grade dropout who received a life-without-parole sentence in exchange for testifying against Glossip—said he'd killed Van Treese at Glossip's request. But Glossip steadfastly maintained his innocence, and he consistently denied telling or encouraging Sneed to commit the murder. No forensic evidence linked Glossip to the crime.[2]

In 2001, the Oklahoma Court of Criminal Appeals had granted Glossip a new trial because of his attorney's "ineffective assistance of counsel." That court stated, "Trial counsel's failure to utilize important impeachment evidence against Justin Sneed stands out as the most glaring deficiency in counsel's performance." Despite the existence of a videotaped confession of Justin Sneed that could have been used to impeach him and the detectives who interviewed him, defense counsel failed to make use of that videotape. "The State concedes the only 'direct evidence' connecting Appellant to the murder was Sneed's trial testimony," the court declared, pointing out that "no compelling evidence corroborated Sneed's testimony that Appellant was the mastermind behind the murder." But in spite of that fact, Glossip was retried in 2004, and a new jury—again finding a murder-for-hire scheme—convicted him once more of capital murder. Before being killed, Van Treese had discovered a $6,101.92 shortfall in the motel's books, and he had planned to confront Glossip about the motel's finances and filthy condition. The motel was in a truly deplorable state, with only half of its rooms even habitable.

As a prosecution witness, Sneed had testified that at around 3:00 a.m. on January 7, 1997, a nervous and jittery Glossip had come to his room and promised him $10,000 to kill Van Treese.

Glossip, Sneed said, had previously made other requests for him to kill Van Treese, with the monetary offers supposedly increasing over time. After his arrest, Glossip was found to be carrying more than $1,000 in cash, some of which the prosecution claimed could not be accounted for by Glossip, who claimed the money came from his paycheck and the sale of vending machines and some of his furniture. Glossip—the son of a coal miner and the seventh of sixteen children—had no history of violence and had never before been arrested. At Glossip's 2004 retrial (though not in the original trial), Sneed had testified, however, that both he and Glossip went to Room 102 after Van Treese was murdered. Although Sneed's fingerprints were found all over Room 102 and Sneed's DNA was found on a $100 bill collected from stolen motel receipts, Sneed testified that Glossip had taken a $100 bill from Van Treese's wallet. At the retrial, defense counsel again inexplicably failed to use Sneed's video-taped confession, though it would have shown how Sneed's story had changed from his 1997 interview to the 2004 trial.[3]

The Oklahoma Court of Criminal Appeals ultimately affirmed Glossip's conviction and death sentence. It found substantial evidence to support the jury's verdict, including alleged efforts by Glossip to conceal Van Treese's body after the murder. A window in Room 102 of the motel had been broken during Van Treese's struggle with Sneed, and there was also evidence that money had been taken from Van Treese after his murder. In its recitation of the case, the Oklahoma Court of Criminal Appeals reported that, according to Sneed, "Glossip took a $100 bill from Van Treese's wallet"; Glossip then told Sneed to drive Van Treese's car to a nearby parking lot and that he would find money in an envelope under the seat; and Sneed—who retrieved the car keys from Van Treese's pants—did so and found $4,000 in cash under the seat. Glossip also reportedly directed Sneed to pick up glass that had fallen on the sidewalk and then helped Sneed hang a shower curtain over the broken window and cover Van Treese's body. Glossip supposedly told Sneed that "if anyone asked, two drunks got into a fight, broke the glass, and we ran them off." Glossip himself had told the police that he never saw Van Treese's body in Room 102 and had only helped to cover the broken window. While Sneed fled the scene of the crime and was not apprehended until a week later, Glossip was initially taken into custody the night after the murder. After being questioned and released, Glossip was again taken into custody after he began selling his possessions and telling people he was leaving town. It was later discovered that Sneed had approximately $1,700 in cash while Glossip had $1,200. On appeal from his retrial, Glossip unsuccessfully asserted that Sneed's testimony was not sufficiently corroborated and that he was, at most, an accessory after the fact for attempting to cover up the crime.[4]

The April 2015 oral argument before the U.S. Supreme Court arose out of a lawsuit filed by Richard Glossip and other Oklahoma death row inmates. The suit alleged that the state's method of execution—lethal injection—violated the U.S. Constitution's Eighth Amendment because it created an unacceptable risk of severe pain. The case was originally captioned *Warner v. Gross*,[5] but it was renamed after the lead plaintiff, Charles Warner, was executed on January 15, 2015, following the denial of his last-minute request for a stay of execution. On that day, the U.S. Supreme Court summarily denied Warner's stay request, with Justices Sonia Sotomayor, Ruth Bader Ginsburg,

Stephen Breyer, and Elena Kagan dissenting. In an eight-page dissent, Justice Sotomayor—joined by her three colleagues—expressed the view that Warner and his fellow petitioners "have made the showing necessary to obtain a stay." The four dissenters pointed out that when, on April 29, 2014, Oklahoma executed convicted killer Clayton Lockett by lethal injection, he "awoke and writhed on the execution table for some time after the drugs had been injected and officials confirmed him to be unconscious." After the injection, Lockett had said, "Something is wrong." "The drugs aren't working," he exclaimed. It took more than forty minutes for him to die.[6]

As the U.S. Supreme Court considered *Glossip v. Gross*, a repetition of what happened at Clayton Lockett's execution was certainly not out of the question for future Oklahoma executions. The lethal injection protocol that had been used at Lockett's bungled execution was, in fact, very similar to the one planned for Richard Glossip. At Lockett's execution, the three-drug protocol consisted of 100 milligrams of midazolam, a substance to induce unconsciousness; vecuronium bromide, to cause paralysis; and potassium chloride, to stop the heart. Lockett's autopsy showed that a sufficient quantity of midazolam was present in his system to render an average person unconscious, but he moved and spoke during his final moments of life. An Oklahoma report issued in the aftermath of Lockett's botched execution laid blame for what happened on the execution team's failure to properly insert the intravenous line. Instead of entering Lockett's bloodstream, a large quantity of the drugs had pooled in the tissue near the IV access point and stayed there. The three-drug protocol to be used at Glossip's execution, by contrast, was to consist of 500 milligrams of midazolam;

rocuronium bromide, a drug similar to vecuronium bromide; and potassium chloride, which—by all accounts—would inflict excruciating physical pain if the midazolam was administered improperly or failed to render the inmate unconscious. In her dissent in *Warner v. Gross*, Justice Sotomayor had written, "[T]he Eighth Amendment guarantees that no one should be subjected to an execution that causes searing, unnecessary pain before death."[7]

The four dissenters in *Warner v. Gross* had ample and legitimate reasons to fear what might happen at Oklahoma executions in light of the state's track record and midazolam's pharmacological properties. The dissenters pointed out that the U.S. Food and Drug Administration had not approved midazolam for use as an anesthetic because an individual "could likely regain consciousness if exposed to noxious stimuli—such as the injection of potassium chloride." Indeed, at a three-day evidentiary hearing, Dr. David Lubarsky, an anesthesiologist, had explained that midazolam is subject to a "ceiling effect," such that, no matter how high the dosage, it eventually reaches a saturation point in the body and might not keep someone unconscious. That feature distinguished midazolam—a benzodiazepine, like Valium or Xanax—from sodium thiopental or pentobarbital, barbiturates that American states had previously used at executions as the first drug in three-drug protocols.[8] When Charles Warner was executed on January 15, 2015, Oklahoma officials actually used the wrong final drug in violation of the state's protocol. Before he died, Warner had uttered, "It feels like acid." His last words: "My body is on fire. No one should go through this. I'm not afraid to die."[9]

By the time of Charles Warner's execution, the once readily available lethal injection drugs—sodium thiopental and pentobarbital—were no longer available for use at Oklahoma

executions. Sodium thiopental—a fast-acting barbiturate sedative that induces a coma-like state of unconsciousness—had
become unavailable after its sole American manufacturer,
Hospira, ceased production of the drug. As a result, in December
2010, Oklahoma had become the first state to execute an inmate using pentobarbital after its own supply of sodium thiopental ran out. But pentobarbital, the state's chosen substitute
for sodium thiopental, soon also became unavailable as death
penalty opponents lobbied Lundbeck, the drug's Danish manufacturer, to stop selling it for use in executions.[10] In 2011, the
European Commission—an arm of the European Union—
imposed a strict ban on the export of lethal injection drugs. At
the time, an EU spokesman stated, "I wish to underline that the
European Union opposes the death penalty under all circumstances."[11] A European Union regulation restricts the export of
goods that can be used in "capital punishment, torture or other
cruel, inhuman, or degrading treatment or punishment."[12] European countries, by treaty, now ban the death penalty's use during
both peacetime and wartime.[13] They also bar the extradition of
offenders to other nations in the absence of assurances that the
death penalty will not be sought.[14]

The U.S. Supreme Court's failure to halt Charles Warner's
execution was especially remarkable because four justices—the
number needed for the Court to grant review of a case—wanted
to consider Warner's claims but fell just one vote shy of the
five votes needed to grant a stay of execution.[15] As Justice
Sotomayor—writing for herself and her three colleagues—
emphasized in lamenting the Supreme Court's failure to grant a
stay of Warner's execution, "I find the District Court's conclusion that midazolam will in fact work as intended difficult to
accept given recent experience with the use of the first drug."

The four dissenters observed that Clayton Lockett had regained consciousness after receiving "a dose of midazolam—confirmed by a blood test—supposedly sufficient to knock him out entirely." They also noted that at Arizona's July 2014 execution of convicted killer Joseph Wood, he had "gasped for nearly two hours before dying, notwithstanding having been injected with the drug hydromorphone and 750 milligrams of midazolam—that is, 50% more of the drug than Oklahoma intends to use."[16] Charles Warner, convicted of raping and murdering an eleven-month-old infant, had been tried three times in Oklahoma before being put to death. Originally slated to have been executed on the same night as Clayton Lockett, Warner was executed only after an eight-and-a-half month delay while Oklahoma officials tried to figure out what went so very wrong at Lockett's execution. Lockett had died of a heart attack after the execution attempt by lethal injection.[17]

At the April 2015 oral argument in *Glossip v. Gross*, Robin Konrad—counsel for Richard Glossip and Oklahoma's other death row inmates, now minus Charles Warner—was peppered with questions about the state's lethal injection protocol. At one point, Associate Justice Samuel Alito interjected, "Now, this Court has held that the death penalty is constitutional. It's controversial as a constitutional matter. It certainly is controversial as a policy matter." In the lead up to his question, he pressed further, "Those who oppose the death penalty are free to try to persuade legislatures to abolish the death penalty. Some of those efforts have been successful. They're free to ask this Court to overrule the death penalty." "But until that occurs," he added, posing his question, "is it appropriate for the judiciary to countenance what amounts to a guerilla war against the death penalty which consists of efforts to make it impossible for the States to obtain drugs that could be used to carry out capital punishment with little, if any, pain?"

Deflecting the question's premise and focusing on the case's broader Eighth Amendment implications, Konrad answered, "[T]he purpose of the courts is to decide whether a method of execution or the way that the State is going to carry out an execution is, in fact, constitutional." At that point, Justice Antonin Scalia—the outspoken "originalist" and a staunch defender of the death penalty's use during his nearly three decades on the U.S. Supreme Court—jumped in, saying that the other two drugs once used in state lethal injection protocols "have been rendered unavailable by the abolitionist movement putting pressure on the companies that manufacture them." In earlier Eighth Amendment cases, Justice Scalia—along with his ideological allies—had unabashedly defended the death penalty's constitutionality.[18] During the oral argument in *Glossip*, Konrad took note of a new Oklahoma statute that had been signed into law by Oklahoma's governor, Mary Fallin, on April 17, 2015. That law allowed nitrogen gas to be used as a method of execution if lethal injection drugs were declared unconstitutional or became unavailable.[19] While the U.S. Supreme Court has never struck down a mode of execution, it has declared in dicta that any torturous one (*e.g.*, breaking on the wheel, burning at the stake, crucifixion, or drawing and quartering) would contravene the Eighth Amendment.[20]

THE U.S. SUPREME COURT'S DECISION

On June 29, 2015, the U.S. Supreme Court—splitting along ideological lines—announced its much-anticipated decision in *Glossip v. Gross*. By a five-to-four vote, it approved Oklahoma's three-drug lethal injection protocol, finding no Eighth Amendment violation. "In an unusual turn Monday," the Associated Press reported, "four justices read their opinions from the bench in the lethal injection case."[21] After Justice Alito read the majority opinion, Justice Sotomayor read her dissent, followed by Justice Breyer's reading of his own dissent, one joined by Justice Ginsburg. The latter dissent explicitly called into question the death penalty's constitutionality. Justice Scalia then went off script, announcing—after the two dissents were read—that he had something to say. He then said that the U.S. Constitution expressly contemplates the death penalty's use, adding, in a reference to Justice Breyer's dissent, the one joined by Justice Ginsburg, that "two justices" were now "willing to kill the death penalty outright rather than just pecking it to death."[22] "Court watchers," CNN reported of the jurists' clash of views, "said the public debate reflected something new at the Supreme Court." "The U.S. Supreme Court," it said, "opened a larger question about capital punishment when two justices in the minority newly questioned whether the death penalty violates the Constitution." One American University law professor, Steve Vladeck, declared, "The fight between Justices Breyer and Scalia over the constitutionality of capital punishment itself is remarkable in any number of respects."[23]

The *Glossip v. Gross* ruling, like so many death penalty decisions, sparked enormous public controversy. In its decision, the Supreme Court held that the district court did not err in finding that midazolam was likely to render an inmate unable to feel pain during an execution. It also ruled that Oklahoma's death row inmates had failed to establish that any risk of harm was substantial when compared to a known and available method of execution. Justice Samuel Alito's majority opinion was joined by Chief Justice John Roberts and Justices Scalia, Kennedy, and Thomas. Justices Scalia and Thomas—frequent allies on capital cases—both filed their own concurring opinions, with each joining the other's concurrence. The majority's ruling in *Glossip* also drew two dissenting opinions. Justice Stephen Breyer's dissent—the one reprinted in this book—was joined by Justice Ruth Bader Ginsburg, only the second woman (after Justice Sandra Day O'Connor) appointed to serve on the U.S. Supreme Court.[24] Justice Sonia Sotomayor, fresh off her dissent in *Warner v. Gross*, filed another dissent in *Glossip*, one joined—as before—by Justices Ginsburg, Breyer, and Kagan.[25] By then, Justice Breyer had served on the Court for two decades, but Justices Sotomayor and Kagan—the third and fourth women to join it—were relative newcomers, appointed in 2009 and 2010, respectively.[26]

Justice Alito's majority opinion affirmed the lower court's rejection of the Oklahoma death row inmates' Eighth Amendment claim, brought pursuant to a federal statute allowing civil suits for the violation of one's constitutional rights.[27] In particular, Justice Alito articulated "two independent reasons" for that result: (1) "the prisoners failed to identify a known and available alternative method of execution that entails a lesser risk of pain, a requirement of all Eighth Amendment method-of-execution claims," and (2) "the District Court did not commit clear error when it found that the prisoners failed to establish that Oklahoma's use of a massive dose of midazolam in its execution protocol entails a substantial risk of severe pain." Justice Alito—who participated in ten capital cases during his fifteen years on the U.S. Court of Appeals for the Third Circuit before being elevated to the U.S. Supreme Court in 2006[28]—emphasized that Oklahoma had adopted lethal injection in 1977 and that the Supreme Court had never invalidated a method of execution.[29]

An appointee of President George W. Bush, Justice Alito had defended the constitutionality of capital punishment in prior cases.[30] In his majority opinion in *Glossip*, he continued that approach, writing, "The death penalty was an accepted punishment at the time of the adoption of the Constitution and the Bill of Rights."[31] Alito then went through all of the prior U.S. Supreme Court cases that had rejected method-of-execution claims. In 1879, in *Wilkerson v. Utah*, the Supreme Court upheld the use of firing squads.[32] In 1890, in *In re Kemmler*, it approved New York's use of the electric chair.[33] In 1947, in *Louisiana ex rel. Francis v. Resweber*, the Court turned aside yet another challenge to death by electrocution after a state's initial attempt to execute a prisoner failed, leading to a new execution date on which that particularly unfortunate inmate was put to death.[34] And in 2008, in *Baze v. Rees*, the Court approved Kentucky's three-drug lethal injection protocol, one calling for the use of sodium thiopental to induce unconsciousness; pancuronium bromide, a paralytic agent; and potassium chloride, to induce a cardiac arrest.[35] Of Kentucky's protocol, Justice Alito observed in *Glossip*, "Most recently, in *Baze*, seven Justices agreed that the three-drug protocol . . . does not violate the Eighth Amendment."[36] Alito emphasized that, "time and again," the U.S. Supreme Court had "reaffirmed that capital punishment is not *per se* unconstitutional."[37]

In *Glossip*, issued just months before Justice Antonin Scalia's death in February 2016, the U.S. Supreme Court's five-member majority made clear that they still felt the same way. In approving Oklahoma's plan to conduct executions using 500 milligrams of midazolam followed by a paralytic agent and potassium chloride, Justice Alito highlighted the protocol's safeguards. "Those safeguards," he wrote, "include: (1) the insertion of both a primary and backup IV catheter, (2) procedures to confirm the viability of the IV site, (3) the option to postpone an execution if viable IV sites cannot be established within an hour, (4) a mandatory pause between administration of the first and second drugs, (5) numerous procedures for monitoring the offender's consciousness, including the use of an electrocardiograph and direct observation, and (6) detailed provisions with respect to the training and preparation of the execution team."[38] Justice Alito also pointed to the district court's finding that the 500-milligram dose of midazolam "would make it a virtual certainty that any individual will be at a sufficient level of unconsciousness to resist the noxious stimuli which could occur from the application of the second and third drugs."[39]

But that finding—as Justice Sotomayor pointed out in her dissent—was at odds with the trial court testimony of Dr. David Lubarsky, a respected anesthesiologist and one of the testifying experts. Lubarsky opined that although midazolam could induce unconsciousness by inhibiting neuron function, it did so in a different manner than barbiturates such as sodium thiopental and pentobarbital. He explained that both barbiturates and benzodiazepines such as midazolam cause sedation by facilitating the binding of a naturally occurring chemical called gamma-aminobutyric acid (GABA) with GABA receptors. In the case of midazolam, Lubarsky concluded, the sedation effect—impeding the flow of electrical impulses through the neurons in the central nervous system—was limited for midazolam and only sufficient for a "minor procedure." In Lubarsky's expert opinion, midazolam was not reliable for keeping someone "insensate and immobile" in the face of "noxious stimuli," including the extreme pain and discomfort that would be caused by the administration of the second and third drugs in Oklahoma's lethal injection protocol.[40]

The Supreme Court majority in *Glossip*—invoking the ire of the same four dissenters who banded together in *Warner v. Gross*—further concluded that "the Eighth Amendment requires a prisoner to plead and prove a known and available alternative."[41] Finding that the Oklahoma death row petitioners "have not proved that any risk posed by midazolam is substantial when compared to known and available alternative methods of execution," the Court found that the state's death row inmates failed to satisfy their burden of proof.[42] As Justice Alito's majority opinion concluded, "[T]hey have not identified any available drug or drugs that could be used in place of those that Oklahoma is now unable to obtain. Nor have they shown a risk of pain so great that other acceptable, available methods must be used."[43] In effect, the majority opinion—turning the adversary system on its head—required the death row inmates to prove the viability of a method of execution by which they *could* be executed. Justice Alito's opinion asserted that "some risk of pain is inherent in any method of execution" and that the U.S. Constitution "does not require the avoidance of all risk of pain." "Holding that the Eighth Amendment demands the elimination of essentially all risk of pain," he wrote, "would effectively outlaw the death penalty altogether."[44]

The Court in *Glossip* explicitly rejected the contention that the novelty of Oklahoma's lethal injection protocol made it unconstitutional. As Justice Alito's majority opinion concluded,

"[W]hile the near-universal use of the particular protocol at issue in *Baze* supported our conclusion that this protocol did not violate the Eighth Amendment, we did not say that the converse was true, *i.e.*, that other protocols or methods of execution are of doubtful constitutionality." "That argument, if accepted," Alito wrote, "would hamper the adoption of new and potentially more humane methods of execution and would prevent States from adapting to changes in the availability of suitable drugs."[45] "Finally," Alito's opinion concluded, "we find it appropriate to respond to the principal dissent's groundless suggestion that our decision is tantamount to allowing prisoners to be 'drawn and quartered, slowly tortured to death, or actually burned at the stake.'" "That is simply not true, and the principal dissent's resort to this outlandish rhetoric reveals the weakness of its legal arguments," Alito wrote.[46]

Justice Scalia's concurrence in *Glossip* took specific aim at what he called "Justice Breyer's plea for judicial abolition of the death penalty." In a no-holds-barred opinion joined by Justice Clarence Thomas, Justice Scalia began, "Welcome to Groundhog Day. The scene is familiar: Petitioners, sentenced to die for the crimes they committed (including, in the case of one petitioner since put to death, raping and murdering an 11-month-old baby), come before this Court asking us to nullify their sentences as 'cruel and unusual' under the Eighth Amendment."[47] "The response," Scalia added, "is also familiar: A vocal minority of the Court, waving over their heads a ream of the most recent abolitionist studies (a superabundant genre) as though they have discovered the lost folios of Shakespeare, insist that *now*, at long last, the death penalty must be abolished for good. Mind you, not once in the history of the American Republic has this Court ever suggested that the death penalty is categorically impermissible."[48] While the U.S. Supreme Court's Eighth Amendment case law bars the execution of the insane,[49] the intellectually disabled,[50] juvenile offenders,[51] and those who neither kill nor intend that a killing take place,[52] the Court has upheld the death penalty's constitutionality as a general matter.[53]

During his nearly thirty years on the U.S. Supreme Court, Justice Scalia was a vocal and steadfast defender of the death penalty, regularly voting to uphold its constitutionality and pointing to its use in America's founding era.[54] "I do not pretend that originalism is perfect," he told the *California Lawyer* in January 2011 in defending his judicial philosophy. "There are some questions you have no easy answer to, and you have to take your best shot," he said. "[B]ut by God," he continued, offering a full-throated defense of executions, "we have an answer to a lot of stuff," including "the most controversial: whether the death penalty is unconstitutional." "I don't even have to read the briefs, for Pete's sake," he emphasized of cases challenging the death penalty's constitutionality.[55] Scalia himself once wrote, "It is entirely clear that capital punishment, which was widely in use in 1791, does not violate the abstract moral principle of the Eighth Amendment."[56] Surprisingly, in 2015, at a talk at the University of Minnesota Law School, Scalia admitted that "it wouldn't surprise" him if the death penalty were to "fall."[57]

In support of his originalist stance, Justice Scalia frequently cited the U.S. Constitution's Fifth Amendment and a 1790 act of Congress. That act, passed the year before the ratification of the U.S. Bill of Rights, provided that treason, murder, piracy, and other felonies "shall" be punished by death.[58] The Fifth Amendment, part of the Bill of Rights adopted to *protect* individual rights at a time when the mandatory death penalty was still in use, reads, "No person shall be held to answer for a capital, or otherwise infamous crime, unless on a presentment or indictment of a grand jury . . . ; nor shall any person be subject for the same offense to be twice put in jeopardy of life or limb; . . . nor be deprived of life, liberty, or property, without due process of law." "For me," Scalia wrote, "the constitutionality of the death penalty is not a difficult, soul-wrenching question." As Scalia observed, "It was clearly permitted when the Eighth Amendment was adopted. And so it is clearly permitted today." Before his death, Scalia professed, "The Eighth Amendment is addressed to always-and-everywhere 'cruel' punishments, such as the rack and the thumbscrew."[59]

Of course, the rack and the thumbscrew—as well as various *nonlethal* corporal punishments like branding and public lashing (commonly inflicted in America's founding era)—are no longer in use in America's penal system.[60] In colonial and early America, offenders were branded with letters (*M* for manslaughter, *P* for perjurer, *T* for thief, etc.), while lashing came to be closely associated with slavery.[61] In 1988, Justice Scalia, wrestling with that reality and its implications for his judicial philosophy, called himself a "faint-hearted originalist" because of his unwillingness to go back to the days of public lashing and branding.[62] But in 2013, he repudiated that concession to those, like Justice Breyer, who—while cognizant of the importance of history—do not embrace originalism. As Scalia said then of flogging, "And what I would say now is, yes, if a state enacted a law permitting flogging, it is immensely stupid, but it is not unconstitutional." "A lot of stuff that's stupid is not unconstitutional," he added, relaying this anecdote, "I gave a talk once where I said they ought

to pass out to all federal judges a stamp, and the stamp says—
Whack! [*Pounds his fist.*]—STUPID BUT CONSTITUTIONAL.
Whack! [*Pounds again.*] STUPID BUT CONSTITUTIONAL.
Whack! STUPID BUT CONSTITUTIONAL. . . . [*Laughs.*] And
then somebody sent me one."[63]

In his concurrence in *Glossip*, Justice Scalia repeated his
standard, eighteenth-century-centric line of argument regarding
capital punishment. After quoting provisions of the U.S. Constitution's Fifth Amendment, Scalia wrote, "Nevertheless, today
Justice Breyer takes on the role of the abolitionists in this long-
running drama, arguing that the text of the Constitution and two
centuries of history must yield to his '20 years of experience on
this Court,' and inviting full briefing on the continued permissibility of capital punishment."[64] "Historically," Scalia contended, "the Eighth Amendment was understood to bar only
those punishments that added 'terror, pain, or disgrace' to an
otherwise permissible capital sentence." Rebuking Justice Breyer's approach, Scalia asserted, "Rather than bother with this
troubling detail, Justice Breyer elects to contort the constitutional text. Redefining 'cruel' to mean 'unreliable,' 'arbitrary,' or
causing 'excessive delays,' and 'unusual' to include a 'decline in
use,' he proceeds to offer up a white paper devoid of any meaningful legal argument." "Even accepting Justice Breyer's rewriting
of the Eighth Amendment," Scalia wrote of Breyer's dissent,
"his argument is full of internal contradictions and (it must be
said) gobbledy-gook."[65]

Justice Scalia—whom Justice Breyer called a "titan of law"
after his friend's death[66]—was famous for his acerbic, often
confrontational opinions. And his concurrence in *Glossip v.
Gross* fell squarely into that camp. Referencing Breyer's dissent,

Scalia—in openly defending the death penalty—began, "He says that the death penalty is cruel because it is unreliable; but it is *convictions*, not *punishments*, that are unreliable." Asserting that "any innocent defendant is infinitely better off appealing a death sentence than a sentence of life imprisonment," Scalia contended, "The capital convict will obtain endless legal assistance from the abolition lobby (and legal favoritism from abolitionist judges), while the lifer languishes unnoticed behind bars." In responding to Breyer's contention that America's death penalty is cruel because it is arbitrary, Scalia further argued, "When a punishment is authorized by law—if you kill you are subject to death—the fact that some defendants receive mercy from their jury no more renders the underlying punishment 'cruel' than does the fact that some guilty individuals are never apprehended, are never tried, are acquitted, or are pardoned."[67]

In response to Justice Breyer's argument that the death penalty is cruel because inmates are subjected to long periods of time on death row and that the delay undermines the punishment's penological justifications, Justice Scalia did not mince words. "The first point is nonsense," he wrote. "Life without parole," he maintained, "is an even lengthier period than the wait on death row; and if the objection is that death row is a more confining environment, the solution should be modifying the environment rather than abolishing the death penalty."[68] While early American executions took place very quickly after sentencing, often in a matter of days or weeks, those sentenced to death can now expect to languish on death row for years or even decades.[69] In replying to Breyer's contention that "whatever interest in retribution might be served by the death penalty as currently administered . . . can be served almost as well by a sentence of life in prison without parole,"[70] Scalia bluntly retorted, "My goodness. If he thinks the death penalty not much more harsh (and hence not much more retributive), why is he so keen to get rid of it?" As Scalia's concurrence continued, "With all due respect, whether the death penalty and life imprisonment constitute more-or-less equivalent retribution is a question far above the judiciary's pay grade."[71]

In confronting his friend and colleague, Scalia wrote, "Perhaps Justice Breyer is more forgiving—or more enlightened—than those who, like Kant, believe that death is the only just punishment for taking a life. I would not presume to tell parents whose life has been forever altered by the brutal murder of a child that life imprisonment is punishment enough."[72] After articulating his view (in opposition to Breyer's) that the death penalty "very likely" has a "significant" deterrent effect, Scalia then emphasized, "But we federal judges live in a world apart from the vast majority of Americans. After work, we retire to homes in placid suburbia or to high-rise co-ops with guards at the door. We are not confronted with the threat of violence that is ever present in many Americans' everyday lives." Scalia's argument: "The suggestion that the incremental deterrent effect of capital punishment does not seem 'significant' reflects, it seems to me, a let-them-eat-cake obliviousness to the needs of others. Let the People decide how much incremental deterrence is appropriate."[73]

As to the now extraordinarily long delays in carrying out U.S. death sentences, Justice Scalia called this "a problem of the Court's own making." "As Justice Breyer concedes," Scalia observed, "for more than 160 years, capital sentences were carried out in an average of two years or less. But by 2014, he tells us, it took an average of 18 years to carry out a death sentence."[74]

"What happened in the intervening years?" Justice Scalia mused, offering this explanation: "Nothing other than the proliferation of labyrinthine restrictions on capital punishment, promulgated by this Court under an interpretation of the Eighth Amendment that empowered it to divine 'the evolving standards of decency that mark the progress of a maturing society'—a task for which we are eminently ill suited."[75] Taking heart-felt, if ideologically driven aim at his regular, constitutional law sparring partner, Scalia emphasized, "Indeed, for the past two decades, Justice Breyer has been the Drum Major in this parade. His invocation of the resultant delay as grounds for abolishing the death penalty calls to mind the man sentenced to death for killing his parents, who pleads mercy on the ground that he is an orphan."[76]

For years, Justice Breyer had been raising the issue of prolonged delays in carrying out executions. In a dissent in 2007, Breyer had written of one inmate, Joe Smith, who "was sentenced to death 30 years ago." "In my view," Breyer observed, "Smith can reasonably claim that his execution at this late date would be 'unusual.'" As Breyer wrote in his dissent in *Smith v. Arizona*, "I am unaware of other executions that have taken place after so long a delay, particularly when much of the delay at issue seems due to constitutionally defective sentencing proceedings." Due to constitutional error, the Arizona courts had set aside Smith's first death sentence in 1979. The federal courts had set aside a second death sentence in 1999 for ineffective assistance of counsel, but Smith had been sentenced to death yet again in 2004. After addressing Smith's extended time on death row, Breyer added, "And whether it is 'cruel' to keep an individual for decades on death row or otherwise under threat of imminent execution raises a serious constitutional question." Justice Breyer pointed out that in a 1995 dissent in *Lackey v. Texas*, Justice John Paul Stevens had raised similar concerns about the constitutionality of a seventeen-year stay on death row. In *Lackey*, Justice Stevens wrote, "Such a delay, if it ever occurred, certainly would have been rare in 1789, and thus the practice of the Framers would not justify a denial of petitioner's claim." "Petitioner's argument," Stevens observed, "draws further strength from conclusions by English jurists that 'execution after inordinate delay would have infringed the prohibition against cruel and unusual punishments to be found in section 10 of the Bill of Rights 1689.' "[77]

The legal battles over America's death penalty have raged for more than two centuries, with the United Nations now leading a worldwide movement to abolish capital punishment completely.[78] In the United States, the last fifty years have seen many major shifts and developments, including before the nation's highest court. In 1971, in *McGautha v. California*, the U.S. Supreme Court rejected a due process challenge to a death penalty law that failed to guide the jury's discretion. "In light of history, experience, and the present limitations of human knowledge," the Court ruled, "we find it quite impossible to say that committing to the untrammeled discretion of the jury the power to pronounce life or death in capital cases is offensive to anything in the Constitution."[79] But in 1972, in *Furman v. Georgia*, the Court found American death penalty laws—as then applied—violated the Eighth and Fourteenth Amendments.[80] After thirty-five U.S. states reenacted death penalty statutes, however, the Court reversed course yet again, ruling in 1976 in *Gregg v. Georgia* and two companion cases that executions are constitutional.[81] As the Court wrote in its judgment in *Gregg*, "We now hold that the punishment of death does not invariably violate the Constitution."[82]

In criticizing the U.S. Supreme Court's Eighth Amendment jurisprudence, and Justice Breyer's stance in particular, Justice Scalia's concurrence in *Glossip* questioned the very legitimacy of the Court's own precedents. "Amplifying the surrealism of his argument," Scalia continued, "Justice Breyer uses the fact that many States have abandoned capital punishment—have abandoned it *precisely because of* the costs those suspect decisions have imposed—to conclude that it is now 'unusual.'"[83] After condemning the "evolving standards of decency" test laid down by the U.S. Supreme Court in 1958 in *Trop v. Dulles*, Scalia offered this parting shot: "If we were to travel down the path that Justice Breyer sets out for us and once again consider the constitutionality of the death penalty, I would ask that counsel also brief whether our cases that have abandoned the historical understanding of the Eighth Amendment, beginning with *Trop*, should be overruled." Of *Trop*, Scalia wrote, "That case has caused more mischief to our jurisprudence, to our federal system, and to our society than any other that comes to mind."[84]

Although history will be the ultimate arbiter and judge of the American death penalty, Justice Scalia—while on the bench—adamantly insisted on that punishment's legality because of its long-standing and eighteenth-century use. "Justice Breyer's dissent," Scalia concluded, "is the living refutation of *Trop*'s assumption that this Court has the capacity to recognize 'evolving standards of decency.'" In *Trop*, the Supreme Court held that Congress exceeded its powers in passing a federal law authorizing a U.S. deserter to be stripped of his American citizenship. "It is punishment more primitive than torture," the Court ruled in *Trop*, noting that "the expatriate has lost the right to have rights."[85] As Scalia contended in his concurrence in *Glossip*, "Time and again, the People have voted to exact the death penalty as punishment for the most serious of crimes. Time and again, this Court has upheld that decision. And time and again, a vocal minority of this Court has insisted that things have 'changed radically,' and has sought to replace the judgments of the People with their own standards of decency." Justice Scalia's position: "Capital punishment presents moral questions that philosophers, theologians, and statesmen have grappled with for millennia. The Framers of our Constitution disagreed bitterly on the matter. For that reason, they handled it the same way they handled many other controversial issues: they left it to the People to decide." "By arrogating to himself the power to overturn that decision," Scalia needled his colleague, "Justice Breyer does not just reject the death penalty, he rejects the Enlightenment."[86]

In his own concurrence, one Scalia joined, Justice Clarence Thomas also wrote separately "to respond to Justice Breyer's dissent questioning the constitutionality of the death penalty generally." Like Scalia, Thomas has been a firm defender of capital sentences during his Supreme Court tenure. Justices Thomas and Scalia, for example, voted in favor of allowing juveniles and the intellectually disabled to be executed.[87] "No more need be said about the constitutional arguments on which Justice Breyer relies, as my colleagues and I have elsewhere refuted them," Justice Thomas wrote, citing various opinions he and others had written in the death penalty's defense.[88] "But Justice Breyer's assertion that the death penalty in this country has fallen short of the aspiration that capital punishment be reserved for the 'worst of the worst'—a notion itself based on an implicit proportionality principle that has long been discredited—merits further comment," Justice Thomas continued, adding of Justice Breyer's dissenting opinion: "His conclusion is based on an analysis that itself provides a powerful case against enforcing an imaginary constitutional rule against 'arbitrariness.'"[89]

Justice Thomas, like Justice Scalia, thus adamantly disagreed with Justice Breyer's dissenting opinion. "The thrust of Justice Breyer's argument," Thomas summarized his colleague's position, "is that empirical studies performed by death penalty abolitionists reveal that the assignment of death sentences does not necessarily correspond to the 'egregiousness' of the crimes, but instead appears to be correlated to 'arbitrary' factors, such as the locality in which the crime was committed." Criticizing Breyer's reliance on one study that asked lawyers to identify the aggravating circumstances of murders, and that then asked law students to evaluate written summaries of the murders and assign "egregiousness" scores based on a standardized rubric, Thomas wrote: "There is a reason the choice between life and death, within legal limits, is left to the jurors and judges who sit through the trial, and not to legal elites (or law students)." As Thomas offered, "That reason is memorialized not once, but twice, in our Constitution: Article III guarantees that '[t]he Trial of all Crimes, except in cases of Impeachment, shall be by Jury' and that 'such Trial shall be held in the State where the said Crimes shall have been committed.' And the Sixth Amendment promises that '[i]n all criminal prosecutions, the accused shall enjoy the right to a . . . trial, by an impartial jury of the State and district wherein the crime shall have been committed.'" "Those provisions," Thomas emphasized, "ensure that capital defendants are given the option to be sentenced by a jury of their peers who, collectively, are better situated to make the moral judgment between life and death than are the products of contemporary law schools."[90]

Subscribing, like Justice Scalia, to an "originalist" approach rooted in eighteenth-century history, Justice Thomas saw nothing problematic about death sentences, even those meted out in a geographically disparate manner. "In my decades on the Court," Thomas wrote, "I have not seen a capital crime that could not be considered sufficiently 'blameworthy' to merit a death sentence (even when genuine constitutional errors justified a vacatur of that sentence)." After describing a few of the capital cases—ones involving brutal murders and rapes—scheduled to be heard by the Court during that Term, Thomas lamented "unfounded" Eighth Amendment claims in which the Court—in shielding juvenile offenders, the intellectually disabled, and nonhomicidal rapists from execution—had granted relief in "egregious cases." "Whatever one's views on the permissibility or wisdom of the death penalty," Thomas wrote, "I doubt anyone would disagree that each of these crimes was egregious enough to merit the severest condemnation that society has to offer." Referencing murderers condemned to die or ultimately spared from execution, he added, "To the extent that we are ill at ease with these disparate outcomes, it seems to me that the best solution is for the Court to stop making up Eighth Amendment claims in its ceaseless quest to end the death penalty through undemocratic means."[91]

THE DISSENTS

The U.S. Supreme Court's decision in *Glossip v. Gross* drew two dissents. In one of them, Justice Sonia Sotomayor—joined by Justices Ginsburg, Breyer, and Kagan—emphasized that "[t]he Eighth Amendment succinctly prohibits the infliction of 'cruel and unusual punishments.'" In her dissent, she lamented that "the Court today turns aside petitioners' plea that they at least be allowed a stay of execution while they seek to prove midazolam's inadequacy." As the first drug in Oklahoma's three-drug protocol, midazolam—she observed—was supposed "to render and keep the inmate unconscious." "Petitioners," Justice Sotomayor wrote, "claim that midazolam cannot be expected to perform that function, and they have presented ample evidence showing that the State's planned use of this drug poses substantial, constitutionally intolerable risks." Rocuronium bromide and potassium chloride—the second and third drugs in Oklahoma's protocol—were "intended to paralyze the inmate and stop the heart," Sotomayor reported, noting that because "they do so in a torturous manner, causing burning, searing pain," it is "critical that the first drug, midazolam, do what it is supposed to do."[92]

In castigating the majority's approach, Justice Sotomayor found that the Supreme Court had erred in two ways: first, "by deferring to the District Court's decision to credit the scientifically unsupported and implausible testimony of a single expert witness," and second, "by faulting petitioners for failing to satisfy the wholly novel requirement of proving the availability of an alternative means for their own executions."[93] Oklahoma's new lethal injection protocol, Sotomayor observed, "continues to authorize the use of the same three-drug formula" used to kill Clayton Lockett, even though the dosage of midazolam had been increased fivefold.[94] At the three-day evidentiary hearing at which anesthesiologist David Lubarsky and two doctors of pharmacy testified, Sotomayor wrote, "all three experts recognized that midazolam is subject to a ceiling effort, which means that there is a point at which increasing the dose of the drug does not result in any greater effect." Although the experts disagreed on *how* this ceiling effect operates, Dr. Lubarsky opined that midazolam's sedative effect is reached before full anesthesia can be achieved.[95] In other words, there is a significant risk of an inmate regaining consciousness and experiencing an excruciatingly painful execution.

Justice Sotomayor's dissent vehemently disputed the finding that Oklahoma's petitioning death row inmates had failed to demonstrate a likelihood of showing that the state's lethal execution protocol posed an unconstitutional risk of pain. "In reaching this conclusion," Sotomayor wrote, "the Court sweeps aside substantial evidence showing that, while midazolam may be able to *induce* unconsciousness, it cannot be utilized to *maintain* unconsciousness in the face of agonizing stimuli." The Supreme Court, she determined, had thus abdicated its duty to critically examine the evidence and disregarded "an objectively intolerable risk of severe pain."[96] "[T]o prevail on their claim," she emphasized, "petitioners need only establish an intolerable *risk* of pain, not a certainty." "Here," she wrote, "the State is attempting to use midazolam to produce an effect the drug has never previously been demonstrated to produce, and despite studies indicating that at some point increasing the dose will not actually increase the drug's effect."[97] "As a result," she stressed, "it leaves petitioners exposed to what may well be the chemical equivalent to being burned at the stake."[98]

In his dissent in *Glossip v. Gross*, Justice Stephen Breyer—joined by his colleague, Ruth Bader Ginsburg—went even a step further, concluding, "For the reasons stated in Justice Sotomayor's opinion, I dissent from the Court's holding. But rather than try to patch up the death penalty's legal wounds one at a time, I would ask for full briefing on a more basic question: whether the death penalty violates the Constitution."[99] "I believe it highly likely that the death penalty violates the Eighth Amendment," he asserted.[100] His rationale: "Today's administration of the death penalty involves three fundamental constitutional defects: (1) serious unreliability, (2) arbitrariness in application, and (3) unconscionably long delays that undermine the death penalty's penological purpose. Perhaps as a result, (4) most places within the United States have abandoned its use."[101] Those constitutional infirmities both resemble and expand upon the ones identified in the early 1960s by U.S. Supreme Court Justice Arthur Goldberg (1908–1990), for whom Breyer, then a recent Harvard Law School graduate, clerked during the Court's 1964–1965 Term.[102]

Justice Stephen Breyer has served on the U.S. Supreme Court for more than two decades, and he is the author of important books on American and international law.[103] Born in 1938 in San Francisco, California, Breyer graduated with a degree in philosophy from Stanford University. He then became a Marshall Scholar at Oxford University's Magdalen College before embarking on his legal career. The son of middle-class Jewish parents—his father a lawyer for the San Francisco Board of Education and his mother an active, civic-minded homemaker—Breyer served as an editor of the *Harvard Law Review* before landing his clerkship with Associate Justice Goldberg. His year-long clerkship in the 1960s coincided with the rights-oriented tenure of Chief Justice Earl Warren, who served in that capacity from 1953 to 1969 after ten years of public service as California's governor.[104] The Warren Court is now best remembered for its landmark decisions in *Brown v. Board of Education* (1954), *Gideon v. Wainwright* (1963), *Griswold v. Connecticut* (1965), and *Miranda v. Arizona* (1966).[105] As an associate justice of the U.S. Supreme Court, Breyer once eulogized his mentor and predecessor, Justice Goldberg, as "among the most highly intelligent, energetic and principled men I have ever met."[106]

As a member of the U.S. Supreme Court, one of nine people tasked with safeguarding individual liberties and the Constitution's Bill of Rights, Justice Goldberg vehemently opposed the death penalty. "During his first year on the Court," one author wrote, "Goldberg was troubled by the flood of appeals that asked the justices to review death penalty cases." As Goldberg himself later described his experience, "I found disturbing evidence that the imposition of the death penalty was arbitrary, haphazard, capricious, and discriminatory. The impact of the death penalty was demonstrably greatest among disadvantaged minorities." Seeing an injustice, Goldberg—later the U.S. Ambassador to the United Nations—tasked his law clerk, Alan Dershowitz, with researching Eighth Amendment arguments against capital punishment.[107] Dershowitz's assignment: "On the first day of his clerkship Justice Goldberg asked him to prepare a memorandum on the constitutional issues surrounding the imposition of the death penalty. Goldberg put it to his clerk that if torture was cruel and unusual punishment, surely capital punishment also should be prohibited by the Eighth Amendment."[108] The Eighth Amendment itself has long been interpreted by the U.S. Supreme Court to prohibit torturous punishments.[109]

Arthur Goldberg had long questioned the use of capital punishment. As a sixteen-year-old in Chicago in the 1920s, he had been inspired to become a lawyer by watching Clarence Darrow successfully plead for the lives of two teenage killers, Nathan Leopold and Richard Loeb.[110] After Alan Dershowitz, with whom Stephen Breyer later taught at Harvard Law School, "turned to the books with a sense of mission" and prepared a draft memorandum finding that a case against the death penalty could be made, Goldberg concluded that the U.S. Constitution should be read to prohibit executions.[111] In a 1987 law review article, a then-retired Justice Goldberg described how he became immersed in the issue of capital punishment. As he explained, "In the summer of 1963, during my tenure on the Supreme Court, in reviewing the list of cases to be discussed when the Court reconvened for the 1963 Term in October, I found there were six capital cases seeking review by certiorari. In studying these cases, I came to the conclusion that they presented the Court with an opportunity to address explicitly for the first time the constitutionality of capital punishment."[112] "I thereupon," Goldberg emphasized, "prepared a conference memorandum on this subject which I circulated to the members of the Court for their consideration."[113]

In his "Memorandum to the Conference," Goldberg—trying to educate his colleagues—proposed considering this issue: "Whether, and under what circumstances, the imposition of the death penalty is proscribed by the Eighth and Fourteenth Amendments to the United States Constitution." "The Goldberg memorandum is virtually the draft of an opinion striking down the death penalty as cruel and unusual punishment," one historian, Bernard Schwartz, later observed. Drawing from the U.S. Supreme Court's opinion in *Trop v. Dulles*, the 1958 case establishing the "evolving standards of decency that mark the progress of a maturing society" as the test for evaluating

Eighth Amendment claims, the memo asserted that those evolving standards "now condemn as barbaric and inhuman the deliberate institutionalized taking of human life by the state." Goldberg believed that the government must show "an overriding necessity before it can take human life." And in support of that view, he cited the preamble to a 1794 Pennsylvania statute that declared, "[T]he punishment of death ought never to be inflicted, where it is not *absolutely necessary* to the public safety."[114] Given the availability of prison and incarceration, Goldberg's memo contended that "a less severe" judicial sanction than death "can as effectively achieve the permissible ends of punishment."[115] His conclusion: executions are "cruel and unusual punishments" in violation of the Eighth and Fourteenth Amendments.[116]

The Eighth Amendment, ratified in 1791 as part of the U.S. Bill of Rights, prohibits "excessive" bail and fines as well as "cruel and unusual punishments." It was modeled on two earlier legal instruments—the English Bill of Rights of 1689 and the Virginia Declaration of Rights of 1776—that also prohibited "cruel and unusual punishments."[117] The former was a by-product of the Glorious Revolution of 1688, a revolution that overthrew King James II of England, a Catholic, and installed Dutch stadtholder William III of Orange-Nassau and his wife, Mary II, as England's new king and queen.[118] After being presented to William and Mary in February 1689, the English Bill of Rights was read at their coronation on April 11, 1689, before it passed Parliament—and received royal assent—on December 16, 1689.[119] Drafted by George Mason in May 1776, the Virginia Declaration was unanimously adopted by a state convention in Williamsburg, Virginia, on June 12, 1776, less than a month before the issuance of the American Declaration of Independence.[120]

It was the Fourteenth Amendment that made the U.S. Bill of Rights applicable against the states themselves.[121] Ratified in 1868 after America's Civil War and the Thirteenth Amendment's abolition of slavery and involuntary servitude, the Fourteenth Amendment guarantees "equal protection of the laws" and makes it unlawful for "any State" to "deprive any person of life, liberty, or property, without due process of law."[122] The Fourteenth Amendment was intended to apply the Bill of Rights against the states,[123] but it was not until the era of the Warren Court that the Supreme Court first applied the Eighth Amendment against one of them. In 1962, in *Robinson v. California*, the Court finally took that step, striking down a state law that made it a criminal offense to "be addicted to the use of narcotics." The imposition of a ninety-day sentence for that "status" offense, the Court ruled, constituted a cruel and unusual punishment.[124] Since then, the Eighth Amendment has been read to prohibit a wide array of *nonlethal* punishments and other acts of brutality, including lashes, gratuitous beatings, prison rape and overcrowding, and being restrained and left out in the hot sun to suffer dehydration.[125]

That Justices Breyer and Ginsburg now want the U.S. Supreme Court to take up the issue of the death penalty's constitutionality is a major development in American legal discourse. They have long been critics of capital punishment, but their dissent in *Glossip* went far beyond their prior public statements on the issue and reflect a growing judicial skepticism of that punishment. As recently as 2011, Justice Breyer was circumspect about the prospect of a majority of the U.S. Supreme Court declaring the death penalty unconstitutional. "It is mostly imposed by state law, rarely federal law," he observed, adding at that time, "Only the legislature can abolish the death penalty."[126] Justice Ginsburg has long personally opposed capital punishment and has even called for a moratorium on executions. But she, too, had never before gone as far as she did in *Glossip* in a judicial opinion. "I've always made the distinction that if I were in the legislature, there'd be no death penalty," Ginsburg said in 2014. "But the death penalty for now is the law," she observed in 2013, explaining, "I could say 'Well, I won't participate in those cases,' but then I can't be an influence." Calling the Supreme Court's review of capital cases "a dreadful part of the business," Ginsburg had previously declined to follow the approach taken by Justices Thurgood Marshall and William Brennan—both of whom labeled the death penalty a "cruel and unusual punishment" in all circumstances.[127]

The importance of Justice Breyer's dissent in *Glossip v. Gross* cannot be overstated. Although Breyer and Ginsburg have not yet formally announced that the death penalty violates the U.S. Constitution's Eighth Amendment, their dissent—backed up with voluminous facts and forceful arguments—concluded that it "likely" constitutes a "cruel and unusual punishment."[128] This puts their dissent just shy of the relentless dissents against the death penalty issued by Justices William Brennan and Thurgood Marshall decades ago. Brennan and Marshall voted against capital punishment in more than 2,500 cases, and they often began their opinions by reiterating their joint view that "the death penalty is in all cases cruel and unusual punishment prohibited by the Eighth and Fourteenth Amendments."[129] Given the strongly worded language of Breyer's dissent, both Breyer and Ginsburg seem on track to vote to declare the death penalty unconstitutional in a future case. If they can convince a majority of their colleagues to strike down death penalty laws, the U.S. Constitution's Cruel and Unusual Punishments Clause would finally be interpreted in a *principled* fashion. Right now, the corpus of Eighth Amendment case law has a Dr. Jekyll and Mr. Hyde quality to it—that is, it ordinarily *protects* inmates from harm, but in the case of executions, it *permits* inmates to be *put to death.*[130]

In the past, Justices Breyer and Ginsburg have repeatedly and publicly questioned the states' use of executions in particular circumstances, filing or joining stinging dissents in capital cases. In *Kansas v. Marsh*, in which the U.S. Supreme Court upheld a Kansas death penalty statute, they both joined a dissent written by Justice David Souter in which he emphasized, "A law that requires execution when the case for aggravation has failed to convince the sentencing jury is morally absurd, and the Court's holding that the Constitution tolerates this moral irrationality defies decades of precedent aimed at eliminating freakish capital sentencing in the United States."[131] Just two years later, in 2008, Justice Breyer would write in an opinion of his own, "The death penalty itself, of course, brings with it serious risks, for example, risks of executing the wrong person, risks that unwarranted animus (in respect, *e.g.*, to the race of victims) may play a role, risks that those convicted will find themselves on death row for many years, perhaps decades, to come. These risks in part explain why that penalty is so controversial."[132]

In *Medellín v. Texas*, in which a decision of the International Court of Justice pertaining to the Vienna Convention on Consular Relations was held unenforceable in U.S. courts, thus jeopardizing a death row inmate's life, Justice Breyer filed a lengthy dissent, joined by Justices Ginsburg and Souter. Breyer wanted to send Jose Ernesto Medellín's case back to the Texas courts for further review,[133] but instead, Medellín was executed shortly after the U.S. Supreme Court's six-to-three decision.[134] In a similar case, Breyer—in a dissent joined by Justices Ginsburg, Kagan, and Sotomayor—wrote that Texas authorities had failed to inform Humberto Leal Garcia, a foreign national sent to death row for capital murder, of his Vienna Convention rights to consult his consulate after his arrest. The Court, Breyer emphasized, rejected "the request by four Members of the Court to delay the execution until the Court can discuss the matter at Conference in September."[135] Despite that plea, the death row inmate's application for a stay of execution was denied, and the condemned man—a Mexican citizen—was executed in Huntsville, Texas, soon thereafter.[136]

These dissents were not the only ones to which Justices Breyer and Ginsburg attached their names. In *Uttecht v. Brown*, a death penalty appeal, the U.S. Supreme Court reviewed a case in which eleven days of *voir dire* were devoted to "death qualifying" the jury—a practice permitted by the U.S. Supreme Court whereby citizens opposed to the death penalty are not allowed to sit in judgment in capital cases. In a 2007 dissent in *Uttecht* that was joined by Justices Souter, Ginsburg, and Breyer, Justice John Paul Stevens wrote, "Millions of Americans oppose the death penalty. A cross section of virtually every community in the country includes citizens who firmly believe the death penalty is unjust but who nevertheless are qualified to serve as jurors in capital cases." As that dissent protested, "An individual's opinion that a life sentence without the possibility of parole is the severest sentence that should be imposed in all but the most heinous cases does not even arguably"—as precedents allowing death-qualified juries have held—" 'prevent or substantially impair the performance of his duties as a juror in accordance with his instructions and his oath.' "[137] Since his own retirement from the U.S. Supreme Court, Stevens has repeatedly spoken out against the death penalty and called for its abolition.[138]

With the death of Justice Antonin Scalia in February 2016, and with his replacement not yet confirmed, the U.S. Supreme Court promises to be more divided than ever on death penalty cases. Justice Scalia was the Court's most outspoken defender of capital punishment, but his death creates a question mark as to how the Supreme Court's Eighth Amendment jurisprudence will be affected. If the justices split four-to-four on a future death penalty case, which—it must be said—is a distinct possibility given the Court's prior voting patterns in capital cases, the lower court ruling will simply remain in place.[139] In other words, the nation's highest court—in considering life-or-death appeals—may literally not have sufficient votes to affirm, reverse, or remand a lower court ruling in a capital case. Once a ninth justice is confirmed, that justice's views on the U.S. Constitution and executions may prove pivotal—perhaps even providing the proverbial "swing vote"—in resolving future Eighth Amendment cases.

To make Justice Breyer's landmark dissent in *Glossip v. Gross* more accessible to a broader audience than just lawyers, judges, and law professors, the full text of that dissent is reprinted in this book. The citations in the dissent, however, have been edited slightly and moved from the main text to endnotes. Traditionally, judges put legal citations in the main text of a judicial opinion. While it would be inappropriate for a lawyer to edit the *content* of a judicial opinion, by moving the voluminous citations to endnotes, it may be easier for some readers to follow the logic and flow of Justice Breyer's perceptive arguments. Readers who want to see the support for a particular point in the text can simply refer to the corresponding note. Bryan Garner, America's foremost expert on legal writing and Justice Scalia's coauthor for two books,[140] has himself suggested that all legal citations should be put in footnotes instead of in a judicial opinion's main text. As Garner wrote, "Textual citations make legal writing all but impenetrable to the uninitiated."[141] Although not all judges have embraced Garner's suggestion, it has been done here, albeit after the fact and through the use of endnotes, not footnotes.

In addition to moving the legal citations from the text to sequentially numbered, newly created endnotes, what lawyers call "parallel citations" have been stripped from the citations themselves. For decades, U.S. Supreme Court cases have been reprinted in three separate reporters: the official ("U.S.") reporter and two unofficial reporters published by private companies, the *Supreme Court Reporter* ("S. Ct.") and the *Lawyers' Edition* ("L. Ed.") case reports. In effect, the same case is reprinted in three different places, giving it three separate legal citations with different paginations for each reporter. Because it is only necessary for a lay reader to see one citation, the version of Justice Breyer's dissent reprinted here contains no parallel citations, which would only clutter up the notes. In a few instances, Breyer's references to recent, *unpublished* slip opinions (designated in the original version of Breyer's dissent as "slip op.") have been converted to *published* citations. Also, the citation format for material in the notes (*e.g.*, capitalization, pagination references, the addition of italics) has been adjusted ever so slightly, with no substantive changes. It is only in this very limited sense that Justice Breyer's original dissenting opinion has been edited. The full text of Justice Breyer's actual opinion, as well as all of the substantive information in his citations, otherwise remains exactly as it originally appeared.

Where appropriate, short or extended editorial notes have been added to the endnotes. Indicated by brackets and italics as "[*Ed. note:*]" to make clear that the bracketed text is *not* part of Justice Breyer's original opinion, these editorial notes put portions of that dissent into better context. This volume only reprints Justice Breyer's dissenting opinion in *Glossip v. Gross*, the one joined by Justice Ginsburg. But as already indicated and summarized above, there was a majority opinion in that case (authored by Justice Samuel Alito), as well as two concurring opinions (authored by Justices Antonin Scalia and Clarence Thomas) and another dissenting opinion, the one authored by Justice Sonia Sotomayor. On occasion, Justice Breyer's dissenting opinion comments on some aspect of another justice's opinion in the case. For that reason, editorial comments are occasionally helpful—indeed, indispensable—for the reader to fully understand the justices' exchange of views or their opposing arguments.

To better contextualize Justice Breyer's dissent in *Glossip v. Gross*, it is also helpful to recall the complex history of America's death penalty, the U.S. Supreme Court's relationship with it, and the background of the U.S. Constitution's Cruel and Unusual Punishments Clause. That information—focused on Anglo-American history, the Supreme Court's Eighth Amendment jurisprudence, and the significant events and circumstances that led to Justice Breyer's dissent—is provided in the remaining portion of this Introduction. The prohibition on "cruel and unusual punishments" was imported into U.S. law from a similarly worded English prohibition dating to the late seventeenth century. Ironically, while England—America's mother country and the source of that now well-known legalese—no longer permits executions, the United States still does. Great Britain suspended its use of the death penalty in 1965 and then abolished it completely in 1969. Abolition in Britain followed the 1950 hanging of Timothy John Evans, who was wrongfully accused of murdering his wife and infant daughter on the basis of the testimony of his neighbor, John Christie. Four years after Evans was put to death, Christie was revealed to be a serial killer and confessed to killing several women, including Evans's wife.[142] Justice Breyer's dissent in *Glossip* raises its own serious questions about the reliability of *American* convictions in death penalty cases.

THE ENLIGHTENMENT AND
THE LAW'S EVOLUTION

In colonial and early Anglo-American law, many crimes were punished with death. The English "Bloody Code" at one time made more than 200 offenses punishable by death, and America's colonial criminal justice system was largely modeled on that of Great Britain.[143] In the Massachusetts Bay Colony's 1641 "Body of Liberties," drafted by retired minister Nathaniel Ward and citing Old Testament passages as legal authority, thirteen crimes were punishable by death: idolatry, witchcraft, blasphemy, murder, manslaughter, poisoning, bestiality, sodomy, adultery, man-stealing, false witness in capital cases, conspiracy, and rebellion.[144] Like the English common law, colonial and early American laws made felonies subject to the *mandatory* death penalty; only later did death sentences become *discretionary* in nature, as they are now.[145] Statutes commonly provided that, upon conviction, the offender would be "hanged by the neck" until dead. Only a reprieve or commutation by England's monarch, the U.S. president, or a state's governor could spare the life of a criminal convicted of a capital offense.[146]

But during the Enlightenment, writers began to question the efficacy and morality of capital punishment. In the seventeenth century, William Penn—a Quaker and Pennsylvania's founder—promulgated the "Great Law" of 1682, restricting executions to treason and murder. That colonial law was short-lived, however, for on Penn's death in 1718, it was rescinded in favor of a harsher criminal code, similar to those of other English colonies.[147] Montesquieu, the French jurist, advocated proportionality between crimes and punishments in the 1740s, explaining, "It is the triumph of liberty when criminal laws draw each penalty from the particular nature of the crime. All arbitrariness ends; the penalty does not ensue from the legislator's capriciousness but from the nature of the thing, and man does not do violence to man."[148] Then along came the Italian philosopher Cesare Beccaria, whose *Dei delitti e delle pene* (1764) was translated into English in 1767 as *On Crimes and Punishments*. Beccaria, unlike Montesquieu, favored the death penalty's abolition for murder, although he and Montesquieu both embraced a core, shared principle: that *unnecessary* punishments were *unjust*. "As the great Montesquieu says," Beccaria wrote, "every punishment that does not derive from absolute necessity is tyrannical."[149] Beccaria was the first Enlightenment thinker to make a comprehensive case against the death penalty, leading to brief periods of abolition in Tuscany and Austria starting in 1786 and 1787, respectively.[150]

In the late eighteenth century, America's founders and framers avidly read Enlightenment texts, including *On Crimes and Punishments*.[151] George Washington and Thomas Jefferson bought copies of Beccaria's book in 1769,[152] and John Adams passionately quoted Beccaria in 1770 while representing British soldiers accused of murder following the Boston Massacre. "I am for the prisoners at the bar," Adams said in an opening line, "and shall apologize for it only in the words of the Marquis Beccaria: 'If by supporting the rights of mankind, and of invincible truth, I shall contribute to save from the agonies of death one unfortunate victim of tyranny, or ignorance, equally fatal, his blessings and tears of transport shall be sufficient consolation to me for the contempt of all mankind.' "[153] John Quincy Adams, the son of John Adams and the sixth U.S. president, later remarked on the "electrical effect" Beccaria's words—as spoken by his father—had on jurors and spectators.[154]

Like Montesquieu's *The Spirit of the Laws* (1748), *On Crimes and Punishments* called for proportion between crimes and punishments. But Beccaria's book, in addition to supporting proportionality and opposing torture, also contained a chapter devoted to the opposition of capital punishment.[155] Beccaria's treatise had a major influence on Europeans such as Sir William Blackstone and Jeremy Bentham, as well as on signers of the American Declaration of Independence (1776) such as Dr. Benjamin Rush and James Wilson.[156] William Blackstone, whose *Commentaries on the Laws of England* was highly influential in colonial and early America, called Beccaria "an ingenious writer, who seems to have well studied the springs of human action, that crimes are more effectually prevented by the certainty, than by the severity, of punishment."[157] Bentham, having read Beccaria's treatise around the time he was admitted to the bar in 1769, was so taken with Beccaria's book that he wrote of Beccaria, "Oh, my master, first evangelist of Reason . . . you who have made so many useful excursions into the path of utility, what is there left for us to do?"[158] Benjamin Rush—the prominent Philadelphia physician—would become one of the first Americans to advocate for the total abolition of capital punishment. And he would do so before America's all-important Constitutional Convention at what is now known as Independence Hall.[159]

Americans despised the English "Bloody Code," and—as part of the American Revolution—they adopted constitutions and declarations of rights that sought to curtail "sanguinary" laws and punishments. Thomas Paine—the American revolutionary whose writings inspired the Revolutionary War—argued that it is "sanguinary punishments which corrupt mankind."[160] *Sanguinary*—a word little used in common parlance today but ubiquitous in early America—is, as it was understood in the eighteenth century, a synonym for "cruel" and "bloody."[161] In 1776, Maryland delegates approved a declaration "[t]hat sanguinary laws ought to be avoided, as far as is consistent with the safety of the State: and no law, to inflict cruel and unusual pains and penalties, ought to be made in any case, or at any time hereafter."[162] Pennsylvania's 1776 constitution also took specific aim at "sanguinary" laws. "The penal laws as heretofore used," read one provision of Pennsylvania's constitution, "shall be reformed by the legislature of this State, as soon as may be, and punishments made in some cases less sanguinary, and in general more proportionate to the crimes." "To deter more effectually from the commission of crimes, by continued visible punishments of long duration," another section declared, "houses ought to be provided for punishing by hard labour, those who shall be convicted of crimes not capital."[163]

Thomas Jefferson—one of many lawyers to do so—copied multiple passages from Beccaria's *On Crimes and Punishments* into his commonplace book. He read Beccaria's book in the original Italian, with his transcriptions in Italian, too.[164] And the wide-ranging influence of Beccaria's book on American law is readily apparent in a 1786 letter that William Bradford Jr., then Pennsylvania's attorney general, sent to Luigi Castiglioni, an Italian botanist, while Castiglioni was touring the United States in the mid-1780s.[165] Castiglioni—the nephew of Pietro and Alessandro Verri, brothers from Milan who had inspired Beccaria to write *On Crimes and Punishments*—had come to America to study trees and plants and get a taste of American life.[166] In his letter, Bradford—a close friend of James Madison from their days together at the College of New Jersey (now Princeton)—heaped praise upon Beccaria's book, with Bradford giving Castiglioni a newly printed American edition of it.[167] President George Washington later appointed Bradford as the second attorney general of the United States, and William Bradford and James Madison—the Princeton graduate destined to become the fourth president of the United States—remained close friends until Bradford's death in 1795.[168]

In presenting the newly printed edition of Beccaria's treatise, William Bradford—who believed Castiglioni to be Beccaria's nephew—wrote, "It is a new proof of the veneration my countrymen harbor for the opinions of your famous relative. I should like it to be known by the author of this book, so well received in the Old World, that his efforts to extend the domain of humanity have been crowned in the New World with the happiest success." "Long before the recent Revolution," Bradford explained in his letter, "this book was common among lettered persons of Pennsylvania, who admired its principles without daring to hope that they could be adopted in legislation, since we copied the laws of England, to whose laws we were subject." "However," Bradford continued, "as soon as we were free of political bonds, this humanitarian system, long admired in secret, was publicly adopted and incorporated by the Constitution of the State, which, spurred by the influence of this benign spirit, ordered the legislative bodies to render penalties less bloody and, in general, more proportionate to the crimes."[169]

The impact of *On Crimes and Punishments* on the American psyche is clear. One lawyer, St. John Honeywood (1765–1798), penned a lengthy poem, "Crimes and Punishments," on those subjects—a poem that explicitly referenced Beccaria.[170] In his letter to Castiglioni, Bradford himself specifically emphasized, "The name of Beccaria has become familiar in Pennsylvania, his authority has become great, and his principles have spread among all classes of persons and impressed themselves deeply in the hearts of our citizens." "You yourself must have noticed the influence of these precepts in other American states," Bradford noted, aware that Castiglioni had been traveling throughout the American states on his extended overseas trip.[171] Castiglioni, in fact, would visit all thirteen American states on his tour, spending more than two years in North America and making stops at Thomas Jefferson's Monticello and George Washington's Mount Vernon.[172] Writing of Beccaria's influence in America, Bradford said, "The tyranny of prejudice and injustice has fallen, the voice of a philosopher has stilled the outcries of the masses, and although a bloody system may still survive in the laws of many of our states, nevertheless the beneficent spirit sown by Beccaria works secretly in behalf of the accused, moderating the rigor of the laws and tempering justice with compassion."[173]

America's revolutionaries were well read. And they knew well the story of the Glorious Revolution of 1688 that produced the "cruel and unusual punishments" prohibition in the first place—and that power could corrupt. "[I]n the late eighteenth century," Yale Law School professor Akhil Amar has aptly observed, "every schoolboy in America knew that the English Bill of Rights' 1689 ban on excessive bail, excessive fines, and cruel and unusual punishments—a ban repeated virtually verbatim in the Eighth Amendment—arose as a response to the gross misbehavior of the infamous Judge Jeffreys."[174] The notorious Lord Chief Justice George Jeffreys—a figure who makes a cameo appearance in Justice Breyer's dissent in *Glossip*—ruthlessly meted out death sentences and presided over the case of convicted perjurer Titus Oates, sentenced in 1685 to be defrocked, fined, imprisoned for life, whipped, and pilloried four times a year for the rest of his life.[175] Oates's punishment was called "barbarous, inhuman, and unchristian"; "contrary to" the English Bill of Rights; "cruel and illegal"; and "unusual" in that "an Englishman should be exposed upon a Pillory, so many times a Year, during his Life."[176] A device for publicly shaming and punishing criminals, the pillory consisted of a frame of adjustable boards erected on a post with holes for the offender's head and hands.[177]

The influence of Beccaria's book on America's founders is equally clear, with Beccaria's ideas on proportionality, tyrannical practices, and the death penalty shaping generations of thinkers.[178] John Hancock—now most remembered for his flamboyant signature on the Declaration of Independence—owned "Beccaria on Crimes," and the Continental Congress, of which Hancock once served as president, was very familiar and evidently impressed by Beccaria's book.[179] In October 1774, the First Continental Congress, meeting in Philadelphia, approved a Declaration of Rights based on "the immutable laws of nature, the principles of the English constitution, and the several charters or compacts" of the colonies.[180] That same month, the Continental Congress—as part of a campaign aimed at gaining the support for the American cause—issued a "Letter to the Inhabitants of Quebec," in which Congress quoted both Montesquieu and Beccaria, two icons of the Enlightenment. The letter of Congress read in part, " 'In every human society,' says the celebrated Marquis Beccaria, 'there is an effort, continually tending to confer on one part the heighth of power and happiness, and to reduce the other to the extreme of weakness and misery. The intent of good laws is to oppose this effort, and to diffuse their influence universally and equally.' "[181]

Just as America's revolutionaries railed against "arbitrary government,"[182] Beccaria's name was invoked often and everywhere throughout colonial and early America. In March 1787, just a few months before delegates assembled in Philadelphia for the Constitutional Convention that produced the U.S. Constitution, Dr. Benjamin Rush specifically invoked Beccaria's name at the house of America's elder statesman, Benjamin Franklin. In his talk, Rush called death "an improper punishment for any crime."[183] The Declaration of Independence—influenced by many Enlightenment sources—itself carries echoes of Beccaria's philosophy, famously reading, "We hold these truths to be self-evident, that all Men are created equal, that they are endowed by their

Creator with certain unalienable Rights, that among these are Life, Liberty, and the pursuit of Happiness."[184] Thomas Jefferson, the principal drafter of the Declaration of Independence, owned copies of *On Crimes and Punishments* in Italian, French, English, and Greek, and regularly recommended the book to aspiring lawyers.[185] For example, in advising his younger cousin, John Garland Jefferson, Thomas Jefferson suggested that his cousin read works by Montesquieu and Beccaria, among others. Likewise, in an 1807 letter to John Norvell, later a U.S. senator from Michigan, Jefferson recommended "Beccaria on crimes & punishments, because of the demonstrative manner in which he has treated that branch of the subject."[186]

Even in the very midst of the Revolutionary War, which ended with the Treaty of Paris in 1783, Beccaria's guiding hand can be felt. In 1776, the same year the Second Continental Congress issued its Declaration of Independence, Edmund Pendleton—a prominent Virginia lawyer and politician—wrote to Thomas Jefferson, "Our Criminal System of Law has hitherto been too Sanguinary, punishing too many crimes with death, I confess."[187] In fact, after enduring the bitter winter of 1777–1778 with his troops at Valley Forge, George Washington—America's first commander in chief—wrote to the Continental Congress, "Capital crimes in the army are frequent, particularly in the instance of desertion; actually to inflict capital punishment upon every deserter or other heinous offender, would incur the imputation of cruelty, and by the familiarity of the example, destroy its efficacy; on the other hand to give only a hundred lashes to such criminals is a burlesque on their crimes rather than a serious correction, and affords encouragement to obstinacy and imitation."[188] Washington came to view executions—even in a time of

war—as too common, instead seeking the option of an interme-
diate punishment, something less than death though more than
100 lashes.[189]

By the 1780s and 1790s, American lawmakers were making
strenuous efforts to put Beccaria's ideas into practice. In 1785,
following the end of the Revolutionary War, Thomas Jefferson's
1770s Bill for Proportioning Crimes and Punishments in Cases
Heretofore Capital finally came to a vote in the Virginia legislature.[190] After it failed to pass by a single vote, James Madison—
who pushed for the bill's adoption in Jefferson's absence due to
his friend's diplomatic duties abroad—woefully lamented to Jefferson that "our old bloody code is by this event fully restored."[191]
In 1786, the same year the death penalty was totally eliminated
in Tuscany, Pennsylvania abolished the death penalty for robbery, burglary, and sodomy.[192] And in 1796, New York and New
Jersey also voted to reduce the number of capital crimes, with
Virginia—in an effort led that year by George Keith Taylor,
John Marshall's brother-in-law—doing the same.[193] "Even Congress, in one of the first attempts to create a national penal law,"
historian Louis Masur explained in *Rites of Execution*, "appointed a committee to investigate alterations in the penal laws
of the United States that would provide 'milder punishments for
certain crimes for which infamous and capital punishments are
now inflicted.' "[194]

The influence of Beccaria's writings reached the highest lev-
els of American government, from U.S. presidents, to congress-
men and state legislators, to attorneys generals and judges. In
1793, William Bradford—James Madison's close friend—wrote
a lengthy legislative report, "An Enquiry How Far the Punishment of Death Is Necessary in Pennsylvania." In that report,

Bradford—again invoking Beccaria—argued for the death penalty's abolition for all crimes except premeditated murder. Noting that evidence might later show the death penalty to be unnecessary even for premeditated murderers, Bradford wrote that, in America, "as soon as the principles of Beccaria were disseminated, they found a soil that was prepared to receive them." The report emphasized that every punishment "*which is not absolutely necessary*" to prevent crime "*is a cruel and tyrannical act.*"[195] In 1794, Pennsylvania ultimately became the first state to divide murder into degrees, with only first-degree murder punishable by death.[196] Beccaria's writings, notes one criminologist, influenced "reformers such as John Howard and Thomas Jefferson, as well as Quaker reformers in Pennsylvania, and became a driving force behind penal reform in the United States."[197]

In the late eighteenth century, the most prominent American jurists were carefully studying the ideas in Beccaria's popular book.[198] In 1791, James Wilson—then an associate justice of the U.S. Supreme Court—instructed a Virginia grand jury as follows: "Let the punishment be proportioned—let it be analogous—to the crime." Wilson—a well-known lawyer who played a major role at the Constitutional Convention in 1787—also recited Beccaria's words in another grand jury charge in 1793 in Boston, Massachusetts. As Wilson told one group of grand jurors, a body empaneled to check abusive governmental power, "'How happy would mankind be,' says the eloquent and benevolent Beccaria, 'if laws were now to be first formed!' The United States enjoy this singular happiness. Their laws are now first formed." Noting that England's Bloody Code, as Blackstone put it, made "no fewer than one hundred and sixty actions" punishable by death, Wilson added that "sanguinary laws" are "a political distemper of the most inveterate and the most dangerous kind." Wilson emphasized that "the people are corrupted" by sanguinary laws and that "[i]t is on the excellence of the criminal laws, says the celebrated Montesquieu, that the liberty of the citizens principally depends." As Wilson proudly proclaimed in instructing grand jurors, "How few are the crimes—how few are the capital crimes, known to the laws of the United States, compared with those known to the laws of England!"[199]

Colonial and early American lawyers, trained in English law and very conversant with the Bible, felt somewhat beholden to traditional legal practices and ministers' interpretations of scriptural passages, even as they sought to curtail the excesses of English law.[200] When Thomas Jefferson, in the 1770s, drafted his bill for proportioning crimes and punishments, he cited both Beccaria and a host of more traditional, centuries-old sources.[201] Jefferson's draft legislation showed Beccaria's influence as it sought to curtail the use of executions by dramatically limiting the number of death-eligible offenses. Still, the concept of proportionality that Jefferson used in the bill—one he later rejected— was based on the *lex talionis* principle of an eye for an eye and a tooth for a tooth. Jefferson's draft legislation called for poisoning those who poisoned and maiming those who maimed.[202] But Jefferson—even as he drafted that legislation—had major reservations about this approach, which he freely expressed to a trusted advisor and friend. "The 'Lex talionis,'" Jefferson told his mentor George Wythe at the time, "will be revolting to the humanized feelings of modern times." "An eye for an eye, and a hand for a hand," Jefferson wrote, "will exhibit spectacles in execution, whose moral effect would be questionable."[203] Toward the end of his life, in the 1820s, Jefferson specifically lauded Beccaria, writing in an autobiographical reflection, "Beccaria and other writers on crimes and punishments had satisfied the reasonable world of the unrightfulness and inefficacy of the punishment of crimes by death."[204]

In America's founding period, as well as in the generations that came after those who lived through the hard-fought Revolutionary War, many Americans devoted their energies to replacing "sanguinary" laws and punishments with a new "penitentiary" system.[205] Inspired by Quakers and other like-minded Pennsylvania civic leaders, Philadelphia's Walnut Street Prison—America's first modern penal institution, which facilitated a switch from executions to incarceration—opened its doors in 1790.[206] Prior to that time, U.S. jails and prisons were often makeshift or decrepit facilities, full of vice and disease. They either resembled or actually were horrid dungeons, as was the case of Connecticut's notorious Newgate prison, a former copper mine that housed offenders in the 1770s. In the caverns of Connecticut's Simsbury prison, inmates labored underground and were chained in overcrowded cages.[207] As an 1844 history of the prison notes of its origins, "NEWGATE is the name by which the prison was called in the days of the Revolution, and was so called after Newgate prison in England. Our forefathers, in giving names to many of their towns and cities, also copied from those of their ancestral home, doubtless wishing to make their adopted country wear the familiar aspect of their native land; and in christening this prison after a receptacle of rogues in London, they intended to give to it a prison-like appearance, and to comprehend all of hideous name, gloomy, and terrible!"[208]

In an era of mandatory death sentences and broad support for capital punishment for certain crimes, the U.S. Supreme

Court often affirmed criminals' convictions and allowed those condemned to die to be executed. For example, in 1820, in *United States v. Smith*, the Supreme Court upheld the constitutionality of a federal statute that made the crime of piracy punishable by death.[209] But views on capital prosecutions and executions were mixed. "In a case affecting life," Justice Henry Brockholst Livingston dissented in that case, which facilitated the execution of pirates John Ferguson and Israel Denny in Baltimore, "no apology can be necessary for expressing my dissent from the opinion which has just been delivered."[210] In its first federal crimes legislation, passed in 1790, Congress explicitly authorized the death penalty's use. And the U.S. Supreme Court—while freely acknowledging that societal attitudes might change—refused to strike down death penalty laws. "By the first crimes act of the United States," the Supreme Court noted in 1885, "forgery of public securities, or knowingly uttering forged public securities with intent to defraud, as well as treason, murder, piracy, mutiny, robbery, or rescue of a person convicted of a crime, was punishable by death."[211] With that 1885 case considering whether imprisonment at hard labor for a term of years is an "infamous" punishment, the Court emphasized, "What punishments shall be considered as infamous may be affected by the changes of public opinion from one age to another." "In former times," the Court noted, "being put in the stocks was not considered as necessarily infamous." "But at the present day," the Court observed, "either stocks or whipping might be thought an infamous punishment."[212]

Indeed, it is fair to say that early Americans did not necessarily relish the use of executions or severe corporal punishments. Many lawmakers, in fact, held out much hope for America's burgeoning penitentiary system—and the prospect that state prisons might one day render executions obsolete.[213] "After the United States of America won its independence from England in the Revolutionary War in 1783," one writer notes, "the new states continued the execution regimes they had in place during the colonial period."[214] But that soon changed after religious crimes were abolished or removed from legal codes as capital crimes, and as penal reforms inspired by Beccaria's *On Crimes and Punishments* were implemented. Pennsylvania, which in 1794 became the first state to abolish the death penalty for all crimes except first-degree murder, led the way, but other states soon took their own steps to curtail executions in the years that followed.[215] In *Democracy in America*, Alexis de Tocqueville made this telling observation after studying America's penal system in the 1830s: "In no country is criminal justice administered with more mildness than in the United States. While the English seem disposed carefully to retain the bloody traces of the Middle Ages in their penal legislation, the Americans have almost expunged capital punishment from their codes."[216]

As a result of the American Revolution, early U.S. lawmakers gradually moved away from reliance on capital offenses and corporal punishments in favor of hard labor and prison sentences. As one writer, penning an article for *The Christian Examiner and Theological Review*, editorialized: "Two experiments have been tried, in relation to criminal jurisprudence and prison discipline, the Sanguinary and Penitentiary Systems." Of the "Sanguinary" system, said to be characterized by "a cruel and bloody spirit," the writer explained: "As a system, it has completely failed." "The Penitentiary System," by contrast, it was emphasized, "had its origin in the United States, and trial has been made of it by the principal members of the Union."[217] Virginia governor James

Monroe—later the fifth U.S. president—himself described Virginia's penitentiary, on which construction began in 1797, as a "benevolent system." The penitentiary system, he noted, was based on the idea that "in punishing crime, the society or rather the government ought not to indulge in the passion of revenge."[218] After America's first penitentiary—Pennsylvania's Walnut Street Prison—opened shortly before the ratification of the U.S. Bill of Rights in 1791, other states like New York, New Jersey, Virginia, Kentucky, Massachusetts, and Maryland soon followed suit.[219] Archaic English punishments such as "ducking," in which women convicted of being "scolds" were dunked repeatedly in water, were declared to be unlawful and not in keeping with American values, even though, for example, ducking had once been labeled a "usual" punishment. In *A Treatise of the Pleas of the Crown*, Englishman William Hawkins—under the heading "Cucking Stool"—wrote, "Sometimes called 'Ducking Stool,' the usual punishment for a *common scold*."[220]

America's penitentiary system was not completed in the Founding Fathers' lifetimes, but that system was much studied—and the source of much pride. In the 1820s, James Madison wrote to Quaker reformer Roberts Vaux that "the Penitentiary System" was "an experiment so deeply interesting to the cause of Humanity."[221] In 1823, he also wrote to G. F. H. Crockett, a Kentucky veteran and physician, who had written to ask the former president about his views on capital punishment. Crockett had sent Madison a copy of Crockett's extended essay, *An Address to the Legislature of Kentucky on the Abolition of Capital Punishments, in the United States, and the Substitution of Exile for Life*, which expressly invoked Beccaria's name.[222] Madison replied, "I should not regret a fair and full trial of the entire abolition of capital punishments by any State willing to make it: tho' I do not see the injustice of such punishments in one case at least."[223] In 1827, in a letter to another correspondent, Madison wrote that he was "attracted to what related to the penitentiary discipline as a substitute for the cruel inflictions so disgraceful to penal codes."[224]

The U.S. Supreme Court did not itself consider the meaning of the Eighth Amendment's Cruel and Unusual Punishments Clause until the early twentieth century, after America's founders had all passed away.[225] In 1910, in *Weems v. United States*, the nation's highest court considered the constitutionality of *cadena temporal*—a harsh corporal punishment imposed in the Philippines, then under U.S. control. That punishment, imposed on a man for falsifying a document, consisted of a twelve- to twenty-year sentence to be served in a penal institution. Those sentenced to *cadena temporal* were forced to do "hard and painful labor" for the benefit of the state and were chained at their ankles, with the chains fastened to—and hanging from—their wrists. In striking down that Filipino punishment, the Supreme Court called it "cruel and unusual" and "repugnant to the Bill of Rights," observing that "crime is repressed by penalties of just, not tormenting, severity."[226] The continuing anomaly of American executions is that while such nonlethal corporal punishments are prohibited, the Court still permits capital punishment, a far more severe penalty. It was not until 1958 that the Court, in *Trop v. Dulles*, developed the "evolving standards of decency" test, which, to this day, continues to govern the consideration of Eighth Amendment claims.[227]

Against the Death Penalty

A Postscript

Stephen Breyer joined the nation's highest court in 1994 after President Bill Clinton nominated him to replace Harry Blackmun as an associate justice of the U.S. Supreme Court. At his Senate confirmation hearing, Breyer was questioned multiple times about the death penalty, including by Senator Strom Thurmond of South Carolina, Senator Arlen Specter of Pennsylvania, and Senator William Cohen of Maine. For example, Senator Thurmond—a death penalty proponent—wanted to know if Breyer agreed with Justice Blackmun's then recent pronouncement that capital punishment violated the Constitution. Breyer's response: "In respect to the constitutionality of the death penalty, it seems to me that the Supreme Court has considered that matter for quite a long time, in a large number of cases. And, indeed, if you look at those cases, you will see that the fact that there are some circumstances in which the death penalty is consistent with the cruel and unusual punishment clause of the Constitution is, in my opinion, settled law. At this point it is settled." Later, Breyer repeated his view at that time that the death penalty "is settled law" and that "applying the death penalty in some circumstances does not violate the cruel and unusual punishment clause."[228]

After the U.S. Senate voted to confirm him, Breyer—with his wife, Joanna, by his side—took the judicial oath on August 3, 1994, putting him in a position to vote on death penalty cases—something he had never done before as a judge on the U.S. Court of Appeals for the First Circuit. As Breyer testified at his hearing in response to a question on habeas corpus, "In our circuit, I have never sat on a capital case. I think the only State that has the death penalty is New Hampshire, and it has not applied it, at least not in any cases, so I have never had any experience with this in the death penalty context."[229] More than ten years later, in an engaging 2005 profile in *The New Yorker*, Jeffrey Toobin—a well-known CNN legal analyst and author of *The Nine: Inside the Secret World of the Supreme Court*—pointed out that the walls of Justice Breyer's Supreme Court chambers are lined with hundreds of old books, a collection that once belonged to his uncle, a philosopher and academic. "On a wall beside the shelves," Toobin sketched the ambience, "are photographs of three previous occupants of his seat: Felix Frankfurter, Arthur Goldberg, and Harry Blackmun."[230] Each of those men once occupied Justice Breyer's seat, and each, in his own way and on his own terms, ultimately concluded that the death penalty was wrong or unacceptable.[231]

While Justice Arthur Goldberg tried to convince his colleagues of the death penalty's unconstitutionality in 1963, Justice Felix Frankfurter had proclaimed his opposition to capital punishment even earlier. In 1948, in *Haley v. Ohio*, Frankfurter wrote, "A lifetime's preoccupation with criminal justice, as prosecutor, defender of civil liberties, and scientific student, naturally leaves one with views. Thus, I disbelieve in capital punishment." Before the U.N. General Assembly adopted the Universal Declaration of Human Rights later that year,[232] Frankfurter wrote, "But, as a judge, I could not impose the views of the very few States who, through bitter experience, have abolished capital punishment upon all of the other States by finding that 'due process' proscribes it."[233] After making note of his opposition in that 1948 case, Frankfurter—as a sitting justice on the Supreme Court—then testified against the death penalty in 1950 before the British Royal Commission on Capital Punishment.[234] When asked if he would be in favor of reducing the scope of capital punishment, he replied, "I myself would abolish it."[235]

One of the last judicial acts of Breyer's immediate predecessor, Harry Blackmun, was actually to roundly condemn executions.[236] In his now-famous dissent in *Callins v. Collins*, Blackmun began, "On February 23, 1994, at approximately 1:00 a.m., Bruce Edwin Callins will be executed by the State of Texas. Intravenous tubes attached to his arms will carry the instrument of death, a toxic fluid designed specifically for the purpose of killing human beings. The witnesses, standing a few feet away, will behold Callins, no longer a defendant, an appellant, or a petitioner, but a man, strapped to a gurney, and seconds away from extinction." "From this day forward," Blackmun wrote, "I no longer shall tinker with the machinery of death." As Justice Blackmun—with strong parallels to Justice Breyer's dissent in *Glossip*—observed, "For more than 20 years I have endeavored—indeed, I have struggled—along with a majority of this Court, to develop procedural and substantive rules that would lend more than the mere appearance of fairness to the death penalty endeavor. Rather than continue to coddle the Court's delusion that the desired level of fairness has been achieved and the need for regulation eviscerated, I feel morally and intellectually obligated simply to concede that the death penalty experiment has failed."[237] With his dissent in *Glossip v. Gross*, Justice Breyer—long a skeptic of the death penalty's administration—now appears to embrace the conclusion of his predecessor, as well as the views of many other justices who, while on the bench or retired from it, have been highly critical of capital punishment.[238]

In the debate over the death penalty's constitutionality, it is important to remember that it is people's lives at stake. After the

Supreme Court issued its decision in *Glossip v. Gross*, Richard Glossip was scheduled to die via the lethal injection protocol that the nation's highest court had just approved. But the Oklahoma Court of Criminal Appeals postponed the execution to September 30, 2015, after Glossip's attorney filed a series of motions, one of which requested an evidentiary hearing. Glossip asserted that new evidence showed that Justin Sneed's police interrogation produced false statements and that Sneed—a methamphetamine addict—had bragged about setting up Glossip.[239] Don Knight—one of Glossip's *pro bono* attorneys—specifically emphasized that a drug dealer who sold Sneed drugs before the murder would testify that Sneed "was your basic meth head" and "was constantly using the drug, using it intravenously, stealing from cars, stealing from motel rooms."[240]

In 2007, when the Oklahoma Court of Criminal Appeals had earlier affirmed Glossip's murder conviction and death sentence, two judges—even then—had dissented from that court's judgment. "I believe the majority overstates the strength of the accomplice corroboration evidence in this case," Judge Charles Chapel dissented. He agreed with the majority that the prosecution "presented a strong circumstantial case against Glossip, which when combined with the testimony of Sneed directly implicating Glossip, was more than adequate to sustain his conviction for the first-degree murder." But Judge Chapel found that the trial court had abused its discretion in allowing the prosecution to post summaries of witness testimony throughout the courtroom and by denying defense counsel's "clear and reasonable request to allow these exhibits to be either preserved intact or digitally photographed, for review by this Court."[241]

The new evidence suddenly put Richard Glossip's case in a new light, giving many people pause about whether Glossip's

execution should go forward. In the lead-up to Glossip's scheduled execution, Michael Scott, an inmate incarcerated in a cell
across from Sneed's, came forward to say, "I clearly heard Justin
Sneed say that, in his statements and testimony, he set Richard
Glossip up, and that Richard Glossip didn't do anything." "It
was common knowledge Sneed lied and sold Glossip up the
river," Scott attested. Another inmate, Joseph Tapley, also told
attorneys, "Justin Sneed told me very detailed accounts of how
he killed Barry Van Treese." As Tapley reported, "I'm sure Justin Sneed acted alone. He never gave me any indication that
someone else was involved." "If Mr. Glossip had been killed,
and I had not done anything, I would have felt terrible for the
rest of my life," Tapley said, noting how he had contemplated
coming forward for a month or so when it looked like Glossip
was to be executed.[242]

With this new evidence, and with Glossip's conviction and
death sentence so dependent on Justin Sneed's testimony (as had
been the case from the very beginning), questions about Glossip's guilt or innocence swirled about and drew lots of media attention. More than 240,000 people signed a petition to spare
Glossip's life, and Sneed's own daughter, O'Ryan Justine Sneed,
came forward seeking clemency for Glossip. In 2014, she wrote
a letter to the Oklahoma Pardon and Parole Board that read: "I
strongly believe [Glossip] is an innocent man sitting on death
row." As she emphasized in her letter, "For a couple of years now,
my father has been talking to me about recanting his original
testimony. But has been afraid to act upon it, in fear of being
charged with the Death Penalty." "His fear of recanting, but guilt
about not doing so," she added, "makes it obvious that information he is sitting on would exonerate Mr. Glossip." According to
lawyer Don Knight, who spoke of evidence of Justin Sneed's state

of mind right after the murder, "Justin Sneed was terrified of the death penalty, and he would do anything to get out of the death penalty. And it appears that that's exactly what he's done."[243]

With Justin Sneed—the confessed murderer—serving a life-without-parole sentence, the prospect of a potentially innocent man being put to death motivated many people to act. Indeed, several influential individuals—among them, Pope Francis, Sister Helen Prejean, and Tom Coburn, Oklahoma's former Republican senator—called for Oklahoma's governor, Mary Fallin, to grant Glossip a stay of execution. Pope Francis asked Carlo Maria Viganò, the Apostolic Nuncio to the United States, to press Governor Fallin to commute Glossip's death sentence. "Together with Pope Francis," Archbishop Viganò wrote, "I believe that a commutation of Mr. Glossip's sentence would give clearer witness to the value and dignity of every person's life, and would contribute to a society more cognizant of the mercy that God has bestowed upon us all."[244] Alex Weintz, the governor's communications director, relayed the governor's rejection of that request, replying, "Governor Fallin has received a letter from Archbishop Carlo Maria Viganò, writing on behalf of Pope Francis. The letter asks the governor to commute Richard Glossip's death sentence. To be clear, Governor Fallin does not have the legal authority to do that."[245]

With his execution scheduled for September 30, 2015, at 3:00 p.m., Glossip—still trying to prove his innocence—sought yet another stay of execution. On that very day, just minutes before he was scheduled to die, the U.S. Supreme Court seemingly dashed any remaining hope Glossip may have had by issuing a terse, three-sentence order denying that request. The order began, "The application for stay of execution of sentence of death presented to Justice Sotomayor and by her referred to the Court is denied. The petition for a writ of certiorari is denied." Although the order did not disclose all the behind-the-scenes debate that had undoubtedly taken place at the Court, it did make clear Justice Breyer's position. The order concluded with a final sentence, "Justice Breyer would grant the application for stay of execution."[246] In the wake of the Court's order, a dejected Sister Helen Prejean tweeted, "The U.S. Supreme Court has denied a stay of execution for #RichardGlossip. At this time, please keep Richard in your thoughts and prayers."[247]

Then—as so often happens in death penalty litigation, with all of its chaotic, last-minute maneuvering and arbitrary outcomes—there was a startling turn of events. In spite of the Court's order, on September 30th, Governor Fallin suddenly postponed Glossip's execution for more than a month. "An Oklahoma inmate was just minutes away from death when Gov. Mary Fallin stepped in to bring his execution to a halt," a local news station reported at the time.[248] The additional time was granted so Oklahoma officials could consider serious questions about the state's lethal injection protocol. "Last-minute questions were raised today about Oklahoma's execution protocol and the chemicals used for lethal injection," Fallin said in a prepared statement. "After consulting with the attorney general and the Department of Corrections," she added, "I have issued a 37-day stay of execution while the state addresses those questions and ensures it is complying fully with the protocols approved by federal courts."

The governor's about-face was remarkable, making headlines across the country. Just two days earlier, Fallin—in anticipation of Glossip's execution—had issued another statement saying that Oklahoma had gone to "extraordinary lengths" to treat Glossip fairly. "Over and over again," she wrote, "courts have rejected his arguments and the information he has presented to support them." In that earlier statement, Fallin had concluded: "If a state or federal court grants Glossip a new trial or decides to delay his execution, I will respect that decision. If that does not happen, his execution will go forward on September 30."[249] "Oklahoma Governor Halts Richard Glossip Execution at Last Minute," the NBC News headline blared, with the reporter's story noting that "prison officials tried to go forward with the wrong drug." As that news report emphasized, "The stunning announcement came about an hour after the U.S. Supreme Court refused to stop the execution of Glossip, whose case drew a call for mercy from Pope Francis earlier in the day." As the news report continued, "The state Attorney General's office provided more clarity, explaining that shortly before the execution, prison officials revealed they did not have the specific drugs called for in the execution protocol—which was upheld by the U.S. Supreme Court just a few months ago."[250]

Although a new execution date was set for November 6, 2015, Governor Fallin later indefinitely stayed all Oklahoma executions to allow for a full investigation of the errors that had marred the state's earlier ones. It later came to light that at Charles Warner's execution, Oklahoma had violated the state's lethal injection protocol by using the wrong drug—potassium acetate instead of potassium chloride. And Fallin's change of heart and reason for postponing Glossip's execution was soon confirmed: the Oklahoma Department of Corrections was about to make the very same mistake at Glossip's execution.[251]

Because the Department of Corrections is not licensed to store execution drugs at Oklahoma's state prison in McAlester, the drugs were scheduled to be delivered on the same day as Glossip's planned execution. When potassium acetate arrived instead of potassium chloride, the execution was halted. "Potassium acetate is a food preservative, but today it was a Richard Glossip preservative because he is still alive," a relieved Sister Prejean, his spiritual advisor, declared. As one report about Oklahoma's initial blunder put it, "Authorities subsequently learned that potassium acetate had wrongly been used in the January 2015 execution of Charles Warner, a clear violation of the state's protocol."[252] Potassium acetate—a white salt used in various chemical and pharmaceutical processes—is also used to de-ice airport runways.[253]

The repercussions of the drug mix-up were felt soon thereafter. Steve Mullins, Governor Fallin's general counsel, resigned in February 2016 amid a grand jury investigation into how the wrong drug was delivered. "I have also been advised by my doctor that I need to better control the stress in my life," Mullins wrote. Mullins's exit marked the third time a state official had resigned after testifying before the grand jury. Robert Patton, the Department of Corrections director, and Anita Trammell, the Oklahoma State Penitentiary warden, had also resigned. As one news story reported, "Patton, Trammell and Mullins all appeared in October before a multicounty grand jury that is investigating how the wrong lethal injection drugs were used during Warner's execution." According to that February 2016 news report: "Oklahoma Attorney General Scott Pruitt has said he won't request any execution dates until at least 150 days after the investigation is complete, the results are made public and his office receives notice that the prisons agency can comply with the state's execution protocol."[254]

Richard Glossip still resides on death row at the Oklahoma State Penitentiary in McAlester. He has sat on death row for nineteen years, and during that time, his execution has been delayed four times. Incredibly, he has already ordered three "last meals" and actually eaten two of them. According to award-winning journalist Patrick McGuigan, a senior editor of *The City Sentinel*, Glossip's guilt is still very much in question. As McGuigan has written for that Oklahoma City newspaper, "Scores of intelligent people who have reviewed the case, including this writer, believe there is more than room for doubt about his guilt. Many have always said there was insufficient evidence for conviction. Regardless, information from witnesses never heard by judges or juries has raised serious (and new) questions." As McGuigan explains, "New witnesses stand ready to testify that Justin Sneed"—the actual murderer of inn-keeper Barry Van Treese—"has bragged about setting Glossip up to take the fall for the killing." "Before all that," McGuigan observed, "many of us reached the conclusion that whatever else it is, the Glossip case is Exhibit A for poor defense counsel, and a matter not worthy of the Ultimate Sanction." "The penalty is allowed under the U.S. Constitution and the constitutions of many states, but it is time to put it into mothballs," McGuigan concludes, asserting—much in line with Justice Breyer's sentiments in *Glossip v. Gross*—that America's death penalty "is so broken, dysfunctional and riddled with error that it is beyond repair."[255]

While Patrick McGuigan is a member of the Fourth Estate, the profession tasked with exposing government abuses, Justice Stephen Breyer's dissent in *Glossip v. Gross* is itself Exhibit A for explaining why America's death penalty should be declared unconstitutional. In 1803, in *Marbury v. Madison*, the U.S. Supreme Court famously held, "It is, emphatically, the province and duty of the judicial department, to say what the law is."[256] Over the years, many justices have concluded that capital punishment is unconstitutional or unnecessary. And all justices are, by oath, sworn to "administer justice" and to "faithfully and impartially discharge and perform" all their duties "under the Constitution and laws of the United States."[257] By adding their own voices to the public dialogue, all four of the dissenters in *Glossip v. Gross* have raised important and troubling questions about the state's ultimate sanction. But the dissent of Justice Breyer—the one joined by Justice Ginsburg—may represent a pivotal turning point in America's ongoing death penalty debate. The number of death sentences and executions has already dwindled, and the nation may be at a tipping point as regards the use of capital punishment.

If the death penalty is ultimately held to violate the U.S. Constitution's Eighth Amendment, it will be because of the cogent, principled arguments of jurists like Justices Goldberg, Brennan, and Marshall, as well as those of Justices Breyer and Ginsburg. The future is hard to predict, just as it is hard to know from the vantage point of almost twenty years after a horrible crime whether or not Richard Glossip is guilty or innocent, though new evidence seems to suggest the latter. There are still almost 3,000 death row inmates in the U.S., and if history is any guide, at least a few of those individuals are factually innocent of the crimes for which they were convicted. William Brennan, the late Supreme Court justice, actually foresaw the death penalty's demise decades ago, just as Justice Breyer's erstwhile mentor—Justice Goldberg—envisioned a world without executions. As Brennan wrote in 1986, "With respect to the death penalty, I believe that a majority of the Supreme Court will one day accept that when the state punishes with death, it denies the humanity and dignity of the victim and transgresses the prohibition against cruel and unusual punishment. That day will be a great day for our country, for it will be a great day for our Constitution."[258] From the death penalty's denial of human dignity, to the cruel and arbitrary nature of capital punishment (issues highlighted by Justice Breyer's dissent), the days of America's death penalty appear numbered.

After reading Justice Breyer's dissent in *Glossip v. Gross*, jurists, lawmakers, and ordinary citizens should be more circumspect than ever about the death penalty's many flaws and then recall Cesare Beccaria's abolitionist vision, one articulated more than 250 years ago. That vision was explored, in earnest, by America's Founding Fathers—the ones revered by so many Americans, including originalists such as Justice Antonin Scalia—as they undertook to construct the country's penitentiary system.[259] Lawmakers and judges should especially take to heart the words of Thomas Jefferson, a Beccaria admirer whose own words are now inscribed at the Jefferson Memorial in Washington, D.C. As Jefferson wrote in 1816 in words that would later be carved into stone: "laws and institutions must go hand in hand with the progress of the human mind." "As that becomes more developed, more enlightened, as new discoveries are made, new truths disclosed, and manners and opinions change with the change of circumstances," Jefferson stressed, "institutions must advance also, and keep pace with the times." "We might as well require a man to wear still the coat which fitted him when a boy," Jefferson warned, "as civilized society to remain ever under the regimen of their barbarous ancestors."[260]

———————

On May 13, 2016, Pfizer—the American drug company—announced that it will no longer sell drugs for use in lethal injections. "Pfizer strongly objects to the use of its products as lethal injections for capital punishment," the company said in a statement. The company's new policy, which enforces a distribution restriction for seven drugs previously used or considered for use in lethal injection protocols, means that Pfizer's drugs will be sold to wholesalers, distributors, and direct purchasers on the condition that they not be resold to correctional facilities for use in lethal injections. State correctional officials can thus no longer legally obtain those seven drugs—hydromorphone, midazolam, pancuronium bromide, potassium chloride, propofol, rocuronium bromide, and vecuronium bromide—for use at executions. "With Pfizer's announcement, all F.D.A.-approved manufacturers of any potential execution drug have now blocked their sale for this purpose," Maya Foa, a spokesperson for Reprieve, the London-based human rights advocacy group, pointed out in the wake of Pfizer's decision.

Pfizer's announcement promises to make lethal injection drugs scarcer than ever. "The mounting difficulty in obtaining lethal drugs has already caused states to furtively scramble for supplies," the *New York Times* has reported, emphasizing that "[s]ome states have used straw buyers or tried to import drugs from abroad that are not approved by the Food and Drug Administration, only to see them seized by federal agents." In 2015, the Food and Drug Administration (FDA) confiscated as illegal shipments lethal injection chemicals that Arizona and Texas—two death penalty states—tried to bring in from abroad, making it more difficult, even before Pfizer's announcement, for prison officials to obtain lethal injection drugs. A similar importation effort by Nebraska—one to obtain sodium thiopental from a broker in India—was also blocked by the FDA in 2015. "Courts have concluded that sodium thiopental for the injection in humans is an unapproved drug and may not be imported into the country," FDA spokesman Jeff Ventura observed in October 2015.

Notably, some death penalty states have resorted to using lethal injection drugs produced by less regulated compounding pharmacies that fall outside FDA approval. They have also attempted—by state statutes (*e.g.*, Georgia's Lethal Injection Secrecy Act)—to conceal the source of those drugs. For example, Texas has obtained drugs for lethal injections from a supplier that the state identifies only as a licensed compounding pharmacy. Likewise, Georgia's law classified all "identifying information" about the people or entities involved in the manufacture or administration of lethal injection drugs as a "confidential state secret." As one law professor, Eric Berger, wrote in 2014: "Indeed, as states increasingly rely on unregulated compounding pharmacies for their drugs, the lack of transparency has grown even more pronounced." Because *Glossip v. Gross* dealt with the use of midazolam, one of the drugs to which access is now prohibited, Pfizer's announcement is sure to lead to more legal challenges to America's ever-evolving lethal injection protocols. It is only a matter of time before the nation's highest court takes up yet another legal challenge to lethal injection—or, as Justices Breyer and Ginsburg have called for, to the death penalty itself.[261]

JUSTICE BREYER'S DISSENT
IN *GLOSSIP V. GROSS*

JUSTICE BREYER, with whom JUSTICE GINSBURG joins, dissenting.

For the reasons stated in JUSTICE SOTOMAYOR's opinion, I dissent from the Court's holding. But rather than try to patch up the death penalty's legal wounds one at a time, I would ask for full briefing on a more basic question: whether the death penalty violates the Constitution.

The relevant legal standard is the standard set forth in the Eighth Amendment. The Constitution there forbids the "inflict[ion]" of "cruel and unusual punishments."[1] The Court has recognized that a "claim that punishment is excessive is judged not by the standards that prevailed in 1685 when Lord Jeffreys presided over the 'Bloody Assizes' or when the Bill of Rights was adopted, but rather by those that currently prevail."[2] Indeed, the Constitution prohibits various gruesome punishments that were common in Blackstone's day.[3]

Nearly 40 years ago, this Court upheld the death penalty under statutes that, in the Court's view, contained safeguards sufficient to ensure that the penalty would be applied reliably and not arbitrarily.[4] The circumstances and the evidence of the death penalty's application have changed radically since then. Given those changes, I believe that it is now time to reopen the question.

In 1976, the Court thought that the constitutional infirmities in the death penalty could be healed; the Court in effect delegated significant responsibility to the States to develop procedures that would protect against those constitutional problems. Almost 40 years of studies, surveys, and experience strongly indicate, however, that this effort has failed. Today's administration of the death penalty involves three fundamental constitutional defects: (1) serious unreliability, (2) arbitrariness in application, and (3) unconscionably long delays that undermine the death penalty's penological purpose. Perhaps as a result, (4) most places within the United States have abandoned its use.

I shall describe each of these considerations, emphasizing changes that have occurred during the past four decades. For it is those changes, taken together with my own 20 years of experience on this Court, that lead me to believe that the death penalty, in and of itself, now likely constitutes a legally prohibited "cruel and unusual punishmen[t]."[5]

I

"Cruel"—Lack of Reliability

This Court has specified that the finality of death creates a "qualitative difference" between the death penalty and other punishments (including life in prison).[6] That "qualitative difference" creates "a corresponding difference in the need for reliability in the determination that death is the appropriate punishment in a specific case."[7] There is increasing evidence, however, that the death penalty as now applied lacks that requisite reliability.[8]

For one thing, despite the difficulty of investigating the circumstances surrounding an execution for a crime that took place long ago, researchers have found convincing evidence that, in the past three decades, innocent people have been executed.[9]

For another, the evidence that the death penalty has been wrongly *imposed* (whether or not it was carried out), is striking. As of 2002, this Court used the word "disturbing" to describe the number of instances in which individuals had been sentenced to death but later exonerated. At that time, there was evidence of approximately 60 exonerations in capital cases.[10] (I use "exoneration" to refer to relief from *all* legal consequences of a capital conviction through a decision by a prosecutor, a Governor or a court, after new evidence of the defendant's innocence was discovered.) Since 2002, the number of exonerations in capital cases has risen to 115.[11] Last year, in 2014, six death row inmates were exonerated based on actual innocence. All had been imprisoned for more than 30 years (and one for almost 40 years) at the time of their exonerations.[12]

The stories of three of the men exonerated within the last year are illustrative. DNA evidence showed that Henry Lee McCollum did not commit the rape and murder for which he had been sentenced to death.[13] Last Term, this Court ordered that Anthony Ray Hinton, who had been convicted of murder, receive further hearings in state court; he was exonerated earlier this year because the forensic evidence used against him was flawed.[14] And when Glenn Ford, also convicted of murder, was exonerated, the prosecutor admitted that even "[a]t the time this case was tried there was evidence that would have cleared Glenn Ford."[15] All three of these men spent 30 years on death row before being exonerated. I return to these examples *infra*.

Furthermore, exonerations occur far more frequently where capital convictions, rather than ordinary criminal convictions, are at issue. Researchers have calculated that courts (or State Governors) are 130 times more likely to exonerate a defendant where a death sentence is at issue. They are nine times more likely to exonerate where a capital murder, rather than a noncapital murder, is at issue.[16]

Why is that so? To some degree, it must be because the law that governs capital cases is more complex. To some degree, it must reflect the fact that courts scrutinize capital cases more closely. But, to some degree, it likely also reflects a *greater likelihood of an initial wrongful conviction*. How could that be so? In the view of researchers who have conducted these studies, it could be so because the crimes at issue in capital cases are typically horrendous murders, and thus accompanied by intense community pressure on police, prosecutors, and jurors to secure a conviction. This pressure creates a greater likelihood of convicting the wrong person.[17]

In the case of Cameron Todd Willingham, for example, who (as noted earlier) was executed despite likely innocence, the State Bar of Texas recently filed formal misconduct charges against the lead prosecutor for his actions—actions that may have contributed to Willingham's conviction.[18] And in Glenn Ford's case, the prosecutor admitted that he was partly responsible for Ford's wrongful conviction, issuing a public apology to Ford and explaining that, at the time of Ford's conviction, he was "not as interested in justice as [he] was in winning."[19]

Other factors may also play a role. One is the practice of death-qualification; no one can serve on a capital jury who is not willing to impose the death penalty.[20]

Another is the more general problem of flawed forensic testimony.[21] The Federal Bureau of Investigation (FBI), for example, recently found that flawed microscopic hair analysis was used in 33 of 35 capital cases under review; 9 of the 33 had already been executed.[22]

In light of these and other factors, researchers estimate that about 4% of those sentenced to death are actually innocent.[23]

Finally, if we expand our definition of "exoneration" (which we limited to errors suggesting the defendant was actually innocent) and thereby also categorize as "erroneous" instances in which courts failed to follow legally required procedures, the numbers soar. Between 1973 and 1995, courts identified prejudicial errors in 68% of the capital cases before them.[24] State courts on direct and postconviction review overturned 47% of the sentences they reviewed.[25] Federal courts, reviewing capital cases in habeas corpus proceedings, found error in 40% of those cases.[26]

This research and these figures are likely controversial. Full briefing would allow us to scrutinize them with more care. But, at a minimum, they suggest a serious problem of reliability. They suggest that there are too many instances in which courts sentence defendants to death without complying with the necessary procedures; and they suggest that, in a significant number of cases, the death sentence is imposed on a person who did not commit the crime.[27] Unlike 40 years ago, we now have plausible *evidence* of unreliability that (perhaps due to DNA evidence) is stronger than the evidence we had before. In sum, there is significantly more research-based evidence today indicating that courts sentence to death individuals who may well be actually innocent or whose convictions (in the law's view) do not warrant the death penalty's application.

II

"Cruel"—Arbitrariness

The arbitrary imposition of punishment is the antithesis of the rule of law. For that reason, Justice Potter Stewart (who supplied critical votes for the holdings in *Furman v. Georgia*[28] and *Gregg*) found the death penalty unconstitutional as administered in 1972:

> "These death sentences are cruel and unusual in the same way that being struck by lightning is cruel and unusual. For, of all the people convicted of [death-eligible crimes], many just as reprehensible as these, the[se] petitioners are among a capriciously selected random handful upon which the sentence of death has in fact been imposed."[29]

When the death penalty was reinstated in 1976, this Court acknowledged that the death penalty is (and would be) unconstitutional if "inflicted in an arbitrary and capricious manner."[30]

The Court has consequently sought to make the application of the death penalty less arbitrary by restricting its use to those whom Justice Souter called " 'the worst of the worst.' "[31]

Despite the *Gregg* Court's hope for fair administration of the death penalty, 40 years of further experience make it increasingly clear that the death penalty is imposed arbitrarily, *i.e.,* without the "reasonable consistency" legally necessary to reconcile its use with the Constitution's commands.[32]

Thorough studies of death penalty sentences support this conclusion. A recent study, for example, examined all death penalty sentences imposed between 1973 and 2007 in Connecticut, a State that abolished the death penalty in 2012.[33] The study reviewed treatment of all homicide defendants. It found 205 instances in which Connecticut law made the defendant eligible for a death sentence.[34] Courts imposed a death sentence in 12 of these 205 cases, of which 9 were sustained on appeal.[35] The study then measured the "egregiousness" of the murderer's conduct in those 9 cases, developing a system of metrics designed to do so.[36] It then compared the egregiousness of the conduct of the 9 defendants sentenced to death with the egregiousness of the conduct of defendants in the remaining 196 cases (those in which the defendant, though found guilty of a death-eligible offense, was ultimately not sentenced to death). Application of the studies' metrics made clear that only 1 of those 9 defendants was indeed the "worst of the worst" (or was, at least, within the 15% considered most "egregious"). The remaining eight were not. Their behavior was no worse than the behavior of at least 33 and as many as *170* other defendants (out of a total pool of 205) who had not been sentenced to death.[37]

Such studies indicate that the factors that most clearly ought to affect application of the death penalty—namely, comparative egregiousness of the crime—often do not. Other studies show that circumstances that ought *not* to affect application of the death penalty, such as race, gender, or geography, often *do*.

Numerous studies, for example, have concluded that individuals accused of murdering white victims, as opposed to black or other minority victims, are more likely to receive the death penalty.[38]

Fewer, but still many, studies have found that the gender of the defendant or the gender of the victim makes a not-other-wise-warranted difference.[39]

Geography also plays an important role in determining who is sentenced to death.[40] And that is not simply because some States permit the death penalty while others do not. Rather *within* a death penalty State, the imposition of the death penalty heavily depends on the county in which a defendant is tried.[41] Between 2004 and 2009, for example, just 29 counties (fewer than 1% of counties in the country) accounted for approximately half of all death sentences imposed nationwide.[42] And in 2012, just 59 counties (fewer than 2% of counties in the country) accounted for *all* death sentences imposed nationwide.[43]

What accounts for this county-by-county disparity? Some studies indicate that the disparity reflects the decisionmaking authority, the legal discretion, and ultimately the power of the local prosecutor.[44]

Others suggest that the availability of resources for defense counsel (or the lack thereof) helps explain geographical differences.[45]

Still others indicate that the racial composition of and distribution within a county plays an important role.[46]

Finally, some studies suggest that political pressures, including pressures on judges who must stand for election, can make a difference.[47]

Thus, whether one looks at research indicating that irrelevant or improper factors—such as race, gender, local geography, and resources—*do* significantly determine who receives the death penalty, or whether one looks at research indicating that proper factors—such as "egregiousness"—do *not* determine who receives the death penalty, the legal conclusion must be the same: The research strongly suggests that the death penalty is imposed arbitrarily.

JUSTICE THOMAS catalogues the tragic details of various capital cases,[48] but this misses my point. Every murder is tragic, but unless we return to the mandatory death penalty struck down in *Woodson*,[49] the constitutionality of capital punishment rests on its limited application to the worst of the worst.[50] And this extensive body of evidence suggests that it is not so limited.

Four decades ago, the Court believed it possible to interpret the Eighth Amendment in ways that would significantly limit the arbitrary application of the death sentence.[51] But that no longer seems likely.

The Constitution does not prohibit the use of prosecutorial discretion.[52] It has not proved possible to increase capital defense funding significantly.[53] And courts cannot easily inquire into judicial motivation.[54]

Moreover, racial and gender biases may, unfortunately, reflect deeply rooted community biases (conscious or unconscious), which, despite their legal irrelevance, may affect a jury's evaluation of mitigating evidence.[55] Nevertheless, it remains the jury's task to make the individualized assessment of whether the defendant's mitigation evidence entitles him to mercy.[56]

Finally, since this Court held that comparative proportionality review is not constitutionally required,[57] it seems unlikely that appeals can prevent the arbitrariness I have described.[58]

The studies bear out my own view, reached after considering thousands of death penalty cases and last-minute petitions over the course of more than 20 years. I see discrepancies for which I can find no rational explanations.[59] Why does one defendant who committed a single-victim murder receive the death penalty (due to aggravators of a prior felony conviction and an after-the-fact robbery), while another defendant does not, despite having kidnapped, raped, and murdered a young mother while leaving her infant baby to die at the scene of the crime?[60] Why does one defendant who committed a single-victim murder receive the death penalty (due to aggravators of a prior felony conviction and acting recklessly with a gun), while another defendant does not, despite having committed a "triple murder" by killing a young man and his pregnant wife?[61] For that matter, why does one defendant who participated in a single-victim murder-for-hire scheme (plus an after-the-fact robbery) receive the death penalty, while another defendant does not, despite having stabbed his wife 60 times and killed his 6-year-old daughter and 3-year-old son while they slept?[62] In each instance, the sentences compared were imposed in the same State at about the same time.

The question raised by these examples (and the many more I could give but do not), as well as by the research to which I have referred, is the same question Justice Stewart, Justice Powell, and others raised over the course of several decades: The imposition and implementation of the death penalty seems capricious, random, indeed, arbitrary. From a defendant's perspective, to receive that sentence, and certainly to find it implemented, is the equivalent of being struck by lightning. How then can we reconcile the death penalty with the demands of a Constitution that first and foremost insists upon a rule of law?

III

"Cruel"—Excessive Delays

The problems of reliability and unfairness almost inevitably lead to a third independent constitutional problem: excessively long periods of time that individuals typically spend on death row, alive but under sentence of death. That is to say, delay is in part a problem that the Constitution's own demands create. Given the special need for reliability and fairness in death penalty cases, the Eighth Amendment does, and must, apply to the death penalty "with special force."[63] Those who face "that most severe sanction must have a fair opportunity to show that the Constitution prohibits their execution."[64] At the same time, the Constitution insists that "every safeguard" be "observed" when "a defendant's life is at stake."[65]

These procedural necessities take time to implement. And, unless we abandon the procedural requirements that assure fairness and reliability, we are forced to confront the problem of increasingly lengthy delays in capital cases. Ultimately, though these legal causes may help to explain, they do not mitigate the harms caused by delay itself.

A

Consider first the statistics. In 2014, 35 individuals were executed. Those executions occurred, on average, nearly 18 years after a court initially pronounced its sentence of death.[66] In some death penalty States, the average delay is longer. In an oral argument last year, for example, the State admitted that the last 10 prisoners executed in Florida had spent an average of nearly 25 years on death row before execution.[67]

The length of the average delay has increased dramatically over the years. In 1960, the average delay between sentencing and execution was two years.[68] Ten years ago (in 2004) the average delay was about 11 years.[69] By last year the average had risen to about 18 years.[70] Nearly half of the 3,000 inmates now on death row have been there for more than 15 years. And, at present execution rates, it would take more than 75 years to carry out those 3,000 death sentences; thus, the average person on death row would spend an additional 37.5 years there before being executed.[71]

I cannot find any reasons to believe the trend will soon be reversed.

B

These lengthy delays create two special constitutional difficulties.[72] First, a lengthy delay in and of itself is especially cruel because it "subjects death row inmates to decades of especially severe, dehumanizing conditions of confinement."[73] Second, lengthy delay undermines the death penalty's penological rationale.[74]

1

Turning to the first constitutional difficulty, nearly all death penalty States keep death row inmates in isolation for 22 or more hours per day.[75] This occurs even though the ABA has suggested that death row inmates be housed in conditions similar to the general population, and the United Nations Special Rapporteur on Torture has called for a global ban on solitary confinement longer than 15 days.[76] And it is well documented that such prolonged solitary confinement produces numerous deleterious harms.[77]

Against the Death Penalty

The dehumanizing effect of solitary confinement is aggravated by uncertainty as to whether a death sentence will in fact be carried out. In 1890, this Court recognized that, "when a prisoner sentenced by a court to death is confined in the penitentiary awaiting the execution of the sentence, one of the most horrible feelings to which he can be subjected during that time is the uncertainty during the whole of it."[78] The Court was there *describing a delay of a mere four weeks*. In the past century and a quarter, little has changed in this respect—except for duration. Today we must describe delays measured, not in weeks, but in decades.[79]

Moreover, we must consider death warrants that have been issued and revoked, not once, but repeatedly.[80]

Several inmates have come within hours or days of execution before later being exonerated. Willie Manning was *four hours* from his scheduled execution before the Mississippi Supreme Court stayed the execution.[81] Two years later, Manning was exonerated after the evidence against him, including flawed testimony from an FBI hair examiner, was severely undermined.[82] Nor is Manning an outlier case.[83]

Furthermore, given the negative effects of confinement and uncertainty, it is not surprising that many inmates volunteer to be executed, abandoning further appeals.[84] Indeed, one death row inmate, who was later exonerated, still said he would have preferred to die rather than to spend years on death row pursuing his exoneration.[85] Nor is it surprising that many inmates consider, or commit, suicide.[86]

Others have written at great length about the constitutional problems that delays create, and, rather than repeat their facts, arguments, and conclusions, I simply refer to some of their writings.[87]

2

The second constitutional difficulty resulting from lengthy delays is that those delays undermine the death penalty's penological rationale, perhaps irreparably so. The rationale for capital punishment, as for any punishment, classically rests upon society's need to secure deterrence, incapacitation, retribution, or rehabilitation. Capital punishment by definition does not rehabilitate. It does, of course, incapacitate the offender. But the major alternative to capital punishment—namely, life in prison without possibility of parole—also incapacitates.[88]

Thus, as the Court has recognized, the death penalty's penological rationale in fact rests almost exclusively upon a belief in its tendency to deter and upon its ability to satisfy a community's interest in retribution.[89] Many studies have examined the death penalty's deterrent effect; some have found such an effect, whereas others have found a lack of evidence that it deters crime.[90]

Recently, the National Research Council (whose members are drawn from the councils of the National Academy of Sciences, the National Academy of Engineering, and the Institute of Medicine) reviewed 30 years of empirical evidence and concluded that it was insufficient to establish a deterrent effect and thus should "not be used to inform" discussion about the deterrent value of the death penalty.[91]

I recognize that a "lack of evidence" for a proposition does not prove the contrary.[92] But suppose that we add to these studies the fact that, today, very few of those sentenced to death are actually executed, and that even those executions occur, on average, after nearly two decades on death row.[93] Then, does it still seem likely that the death penalty has a significant deterrent effect?

Consider, for example, what actually happened to the 183 inmates sentenced to death in 1978. As of 2013 (35 years later), 38 (or 21% of them) had been executed; 132 (or 72%) had had their convictions or sentences overturned or commuted; and 7 (or 4%) had died of other (likely natural) causes. Six (or 3%) remained on death row.[94]

The example illustrates a general trend. Of the 8,466 inmates under a death sentence at some point between 1973 and 2013, 16% were executed, 42% had their convictions or sentences overturned or commuted, and 6% died by other causes; the remainder (35%) are still on death row.[95]

Thus an offender who is sentenced to death is two or three times more likely to find his sentence overturned or commuted than to be executed; and he has a good chance of dying from natural causes before any execution (or exoneration) can take place. In a word, executions are *rare*. And an individual contemplating a crime but evaluating the potential punishment would know that, in any event, he faces a potential sentence of life without parole.

These facts, when recurring, must have some offsetting effect on a potential perpetrator's fear of a death penalty. And, even if that effect is no more than slight, it makes it difficult to believe (given the studies of deterrence cited earlier) that such a rare event significantly deters horrendous crimes.[96]

But what about retribution? Retribution is a valid penological goal. I recognize that surviving relatives of victims of a horrendous crime, or perhaps the community itself, may find vindication in an execution. And a community that favors the death penalty has an understandable interest in representing their voices.[97]

The relevant question here, however, is whether a "community's sense of retribution" can often find vindication in "a death that comes," if at all, "only several decades after the crime was committed."[98] By then the community is a different group of people. The offenders and the victims' families have grown far older. Feelings of outrage may have subsided. The offender may have found himself a changed human being. And sometimes repentance and even forgiveness can restore meaning to lives once ruined. At the same time, the community and victims' families will know that, even without a further death, the offender will serve decades in prison under a sentence of life without parole.

I recognize, of course, that this may not always be the case, and that sometimes the community believes that an execution could provide closure. Nevertheless, the delays and low probability of execution must play some role in any calculation that leads a community to insist on death as retribution. As I have already suggested, they may well attenuate the community's interest in retribution to the point where it cannot by itself amount to a significant justification for the death penalty.[99] In any event, I believe that whatever interest in retribution might be served by the death penalty as currently administered, that interest can be served almost as well by a sentence of life in prison without parole (a sentence that every State now permits).[100]

Finally, the fact of lengthy delays undermines any effort to justify the death penalty in terms of its prevalence when the Founders wrote the Eighth Amendment. When the Founders wrote the Constitution, there were no 20- or 30-year delays. Execution took place soon after sentencing.[101] And, for reasons I shall describe,[102] we cannot return to the quick executions in the founding era.

3

The upshot is that lengthy delays both aggravate the cruelty of the death penalty and undermine its jurisprudential rationale. And this Court has said that, if the death penalty does not fulfill the goals of deterrence or retribution, "it is nothing more than the purposeless and needless imposition of pain and suffering and hence an unconstitutional punishment."[103]

Indeed, Justice Lewis Powell (who provided a crucial vote in *Gregg*) came to much the same conclusion, albeit after his retirement from this Court. Justice Powell had come to the Court convinced that the Federal Constitution did not outlaw the death penalty but rather left the matter up to individual States to determine.[104]

Soon after Justice Powell's retirement, Chief Justice Rehnquist appointed him to chair a committee addressing concerns about delays in capital cases, the Ad Hoc Committee on Federal Habeas Corpus in Capital Cases (Committee). The Committee presented a report to Congress, and Justice Powell testified that "[d]elay robs the penalty of much of its deterrent value."[105] Justice Powell, according to his official biographer, ultimately concluded that capital punishment:

> " 'serves no useful purpose.' The United States was 'unique among the industrialized nations of the West in maintaining the death penalty,' and it was enforced so rarely that it could not deter. More important, the haggling and delay and seemingly endless litigation in every capital case brought the law itself into disrepute."[106]

In short, the problem of excessive delays led Justice Powell, at least in part, to conclude that the death penalty was unconstitutional.

As I have said, today delays are much worse. When Chief Justice Rehnquist appointed Justice Powell to the Committee, the average delay between sentencing and execution was 7 years and 11 months, compared with 17 years and 7 months today.[107]

C

One might ask, why can Congress or the States not deal directly with the delay problem? Why can they not take steps to shorten the time between sentence and execution, and thereby mitigate the problems just raised? The answer is that shortening delay is much more difficult than one might think. And that is in part because efforts to do so risk causing procedural harms that also undermine the death penalty's constitutionality.

For one thing, delays have helped to make application of the death penalty more reliable. Recall the case of Henry Lee McCollum, whom DNA evidence exonerated 30 years after his conviction.[108] If McCollum had been executed earlier, he would not have lived to see the day when DNA evidence exonerated him and implicated another man; that man is already serving a life sentence for a rape and murder that he committed just a few weeks after the murder McCollum was convicted of.[109] In fact, this Court had earlier denied review of McCollum's claim over the public dissent of only one Justice.[110] And yet a full 20 years after the Court denied review, McCollum was exonerated by DNA evidence. There are a significant number of similar cases, some of which I have discussed earlier.[111]

In addition to those who are exonerated on the ground that they are innocent, there are other individuals whose sentences or convictions have been overturned for other reasons (as discussed above, state and federal courts found error in 68% of the capital cases they reviewed between 1973 and 1995).[112] In many of these cases, a court will have found that the individual did not merit the death penalty in a special sense—namely, he failed to receive all the procedural protections that the law requires for the death penalty's application. By eliminating some of these protections, one likely could reduce delay. But which protections should we eliminate? Should we eliminate the trial-related protections we have established for capital defendants: that they be able to present to the sentencing judge or jury all mitigating circumstances;[113] that the State provide guidance adequate to reserve the application of the death penalty to particularly serious murders;[114] that the State provide adequate counsel and, where warranted, adequate expert assistance;[115] or that a jury must find the aggravating factors necessary to impose the death penalty?[116] Should we no longer ensure that the State does not execute those who are seriously intellectually disabled?[117] Should we eliminate the requirement that the manner of execution be constitutional,[118] or the requirement that the inmate be mentally competent at the time of his execution?[119] Or should we get rid of the criminal protections that all criminal defendants receive—for instance, that defendants claiming violation of constitutional guarantees (say "due process of law") may seek a writ of habeas corpus in federal courts?[120] My answer to these questions is "surely not."[121]

One might, of course, argue that courts, particularly federal courts providing additional layers of review, apply these and other requirements too strictly, and that causes delay. But, it is difficult for judges, as it would be difficult for anyone, *not* to apply legal requirements punctiliously when the consequence of failing to do so may well be death, particularly the death of an innocent person.[122]

Moreover, review by courts at every level helps to ensure reliability; if this Court had not ordered that Anthony Ray Hinton receive further hearings in state court,[123] he may well have been executed rather than exonerated. In my own view, our legal system's complexity, our federal system with its separate state and federal courts, our constitutional guarantees, our commitment to fair procedure, and, above all, a special need for reliability and fairness in capital cases, combine to make significant procedural "reform" unlikely in practice to reduce delays to an acceptable level.

And that fact creates a dilemma: A death penalty system that seeks procedural fairness and reliability brings with it delays that severely aggravate the cruelty of capital punishment and significantly undermine the rationale for imposing a sentence of death in the first place.[124] But a death penalty system that minimizes delays would undermine the legal system's efforts to secure reliability and procedural fairness.

In this world, or at least in this Nation, we can have a death penalty that at least arguably serves legitimate penological purposes *or* we can have a procedural system that at least arguably seeks reliability and fairness in the death penalty's application. We cannot have both. And that simple fact, demonstrated convincingly over the past 40 years, strongly supports the claim that the death penalty violates the Eighth Amendment. A death penalty system that is unreliable or procedurally unfair would violate the Eighth Amendment.[125] And so would a system that, if reliable and fair in its application of the death penalty, would serve no legitimate penological purpose.[126]

IV

"Unusual"—Decline in Use of the Death Penalty

The Eighth Amendment forbids punishments that are cruel and *unusual*. Last year, in 2014, only seven States carried out an execution. Perhaps more importantly, in the last two decades, the imposition and implementation of the death penalty have increasingly become unusual. I can illustrate the significant decline in the use of the death penalty in several ways.

An appropriate starting point concerns the trajectory of the number of annual death sentences nationwide, from the 1970's to present day. In 1977—just after the Supreme Court made clear that, by modifying their legislation, States could reinstate the death penalty—137 people were sentenced to death.[127] Many States having revised their death penalty laws to meet *Furman*'s requirements, the number of death sentences then increased. Between 1986 and 1999, 286 persons on average were sentenced to death each year.[128] But, approximately 15 years ago, the numbers began to decline, and they have declined rapidly ever since.[129] In 1999, 279 persons were sentenced to death.[130] Last year, just 73 persons were sentenced to death.[131]

That trend, a significant decline in the last 15 years, also holds true with respect to the number of annual executions.[132] In 1999, 98 people were executed.[133] Last year, that number was only 35.[134]

Next, one can consider state-level data. Often when deciding whether a punishment practice is, constitutionally speaking, "unusual," this Court has looked to the number of States engaging in that practice.[135] In this respect, the number of active death penalty States has fallen dramatically. In 1972, when the Court decided *Furman,* the death penalty was lawful in 41 States. Nine States had abolished it.[136] As of today, 19 States have abolished the death penalty (along with the District of Columbia), although some did so prospectively only.[137] In 11 other States that maintain the death penalty on the books, no execution has taken place for more than eight years: Arkansas (last execution 2005); California (2006); Colorado (1997); Kansas (no executions since the death penalty was reinstated in 1976); Montana (2006); Nevada (2006); New Hampshire (no executions since the death penalty was reinstated in 1976); North Carolina (2006); Oregon (1997); Pennsylvania (1999); and Wyoming (1992).[138]

Accordingly, 30 States have either formally abolished the death penalty or have not conducted an execution in more than eight years. Of the 20 States that have conducted at least one execution in the past eight years, 9 have conducted fewer than five in that time, making an execution in those States a fairly rare event.[139] That leaves 11 States in which it is fair to say that capital punishment is not "unusual." And just three of those States (Texas, Missouri, and Florida) accounted for 80% of the executions nationwide (28 of the 35) in 2014.[140] Indeed, last year, only seven States conducted an execution.[141] In other words, in 43 States, no one was executed.

In terms of population, if we ask how many Americans live in a State that at least occasionally carries out an execution (at least one within the prior three years), the answer two decades ago was 60% or 70%. Today, that number is 33%.[142]

At the same time, use of the death penalty has become increasingly concentrated geographically. County-by-county figures are relevant, for decisions to impose the death penalty typically take place at a county level.[143] County-level sentencing figures show that, between 1973 and 1997, 66 of America's 3,143 counties accounted for approximately 50% of all death sentences imposed.[144] By the early 2000's, the death penalty was only actively practiced in a very small number of counties: between 2004 and 2009, only 35 counties imposed 5 or more death sentences, *i.e.*, approximately one per year.[145] And more recent data show that the practice has diminished yet further: between 2010 and 2015 (as of June 22), only 15 counties imposed five or more death sentences.[146] In short, the number of active death penalty counties is small and getting smaller. And the overall statistics on county-level executions bear this out. Between 1976 and 2007, there were no executions in 86% of America's counties.[147]

In sum, if we look to States, in more than 60% there is effectively no death penalty, in an additional 18% an execution is rare and unusual, and 6%, *i.e.*, three States, account for 80% of all executions. If we look to population, about 66% of the Nation lives in a State that has not carried out an execution in the last three years. And if we look to counties, in 86% there is effectively no death penalty. It seems fair to say that it is now unusual to find capital punishment in the United States, at least when we consider the Nation as a whole.[148]

Moreover, we have said that it " 'is not so much the number of these States that is significant, but the consistency of the direction of change.' "[149] Judged in that way, capital punishment has indeed become unusual. Seven States have abolished the death penalty in the last decade, including (quite recently) Nebraska.[150] And several States have come within a single vote of eliminating the death penalty.[151] Eleven States, as noted earlier, have not executed anyone in eight years.[152] And several States have formally stopped executing inmates.[153]

Moreover, the direction of change is consistent. In the past two decades, no State without a death penalty has passed legislation to reinstate the penalty.[154] Indeed, even in many States most associated with the death penalty, remarkable shifts have occurred. In Texas, the State that carries out the most executions, the number of executions fell from 40 in 2000 to 10 in 2014, and the number of death sentences fell from 48 in 1999 to 9 in 2013 (and 0 thus far in 2015).[155] Similarly dramatic declines are present in Virginia, Oklahoma, Missouri, and North Carolina.[156]

These circumstances perhaps reflect the fact that a majority of Americans, when asked to choose between the death penalty and life in prison without parole, now choose the latter.[157]

I rely primarily upon domestic, not foreign events, in pointing to changes and circumstances that tend to justify the claim that the death penalty, constitutionally speaking, is "unusual." Those circumstances are sufficient to warrant our reconsideration of the death penalty's constitutionality. I note, however, that many nations—indeed, 95 of the 193 members of the United Nations—have formally abolished the death penalty and an additional 42 have abolished it in practice.[158] In 2013, only 22 countries in the world carried out an execution.[159] No executions were carried out in Europe or Central Asia, and the United States was the only country in the Americas to execute an inmate in 2013.[160] Only eight countries executed more than 10 individuals (the United States, China, Iran, Iraq, Saudi Arabia, Somalia, Sudan, Yemen).[161] And almost 80% of all known executions took place in three countries: Iran, Iraq, and Saudi

Arabia.[162] (This figure does not include China, which has a large population, but where precise data cannot be obtained.[163])

V

I recognize a strong counterargument that favors constitutionality. We are a court. Why should we not leave the matter up to the people acting democratically through legislatures? The Constitution foresees a country that will make most important decisions democratically. Most nations that have abandoned the death penalty have done so through legislation, not judicial decision. And legislators, unlike judges, are free to take account of matters such as monetary costs, which I do not claim are relevant here.[164]

The answer is that the matters I have discussed, such as lack of reliability, the arbitrary application of a serious and irreversible punishment, individual suffering caused by long delays, and lack of penological purpose are quintessentially judicial matters. They concern the infliction—indeed the unfair, cruel, and unusual infliction—of a serious punishment upon an individual. I recognize that in 1972 this Court, in a sense, turned to Congress and the state legislatures in its search for standards that would increase the fairness and reliability of imposing a death penalty. The legislatures responded. But, in the last four decades, considerable evidence has accumulated that those responses have not worked.

Thus we are left with a judicial responsibility. The Eighth Amendment sets forth the relevant law, and we must interpret that law.[165] We have made clear that " 'the Constitution contemplates that in the end our own judgment will be brought to bear on the question of the acceptability of the death penalty under the Eighth Amendment.' "[166]

For the reasons I have set forth in this opinion, I believe it highly likely that the death penalty violates the Eighth Amendment. At the very least, the Court should call for full briefing on the basic question.

With respect, I dissent.

APPENDIX A

Death Sentences Imposed, 1977–2014

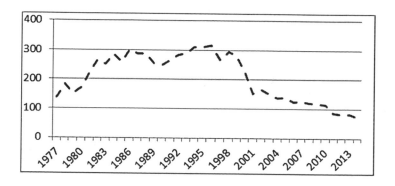

APPENDIX B

Executions, 1977–2014

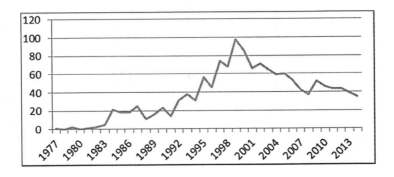

Percentage of U.S. Population in States that Conducted an Execution within Prior Three Years

Year	Percentage	Year	Percentage
1994	54	2005	52
1995	60	2006	55
1996	63	2007	57
1997	63	2008	53
1998	61	2009	39
1999	70	2010	43
2000	68	2011	42
2001	67	2012	39
2002	57	2013	34
2003	53	2014	33
2004	52		

APPENDIX D

Counties with Death Sentences, 2004–2009

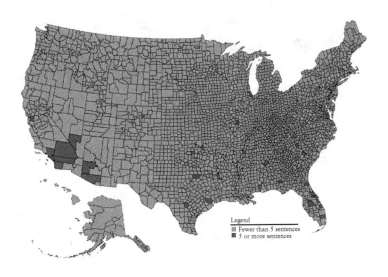

Source: Ford, The Death Penalty's Last Stand, *The Atlantic*, April 21, 2015.

APPENDIX E

Counties with Death Sentences, 2010–Present

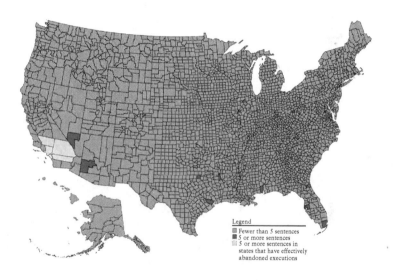

Legend
Fewer than 5 sentences
5 or more sentences
5 or more sentences in states that have effectively abandoned executions

Source: The underlying data was compiled with research assistance from the Supreme Court Library (current as of June 22, 2015).

NOTES

1. Transcript of Oral Argument, *Richard E. Glossip, et al. v. Kevin J. Gross, et al.*, No. 14-7955 (U.S. Supreme Court), at www.supremecourt.gov/oral_arguments/argument_transcripts/14-7955_1b72.pdf. [*Ed. note:* This book's editor expresses his gratitude to two University of Baltimore law students, Valerie Bonk and Alex Powell, for their superb research assistance.]

2. *Glossip v. State of Oklahoma*, 29 P.3d 597, 598 (Okla. Ct. Crim. App. 2001); *Glossip v. State of Oklahoma*, 157 P.3d 143, 148–53 (Okla. Ct. Crim. App. 2007); *Glossip v. Workman*, No. CIV-08-0326-HE, 2010 WL 2196110 *1 (W.D. Okla., May 26, 2010); Samantha Vicent, Richard Glossip Case: Here's the Story of His Victim, Tulsa World, Sept. 7, 2015, at www.tulsaworld.com/news/courts/richard-glossip-case-here-is-the-story-of-his-victim/article_1247f4c4-a8be-5492-b438-1c5d39c8b571.html.

3. Richard Glossip Talking Points, at www.sisterhelen.org/wordpress/wp-content/uploads/Richard_Glossip_talking_points.pdf.

4. *Glossip*, 29 P.3d at 598–603; *Glossip*, 157 P.3d at 147–64; *id.* at 173 (Chapel, J., dissenting). Initially, the state of Oklahoma charged Richard Glossip with being an accessory after the fact to murder, but then it dismissed the accessory information and added Glossip as a

codefendant with Sneed on the murder charge. *Id.* at 157. In his 2001 appeal, Glossip had successfully argued that he was entitled to a jury instruction on the crime of accessory after the fact. *Glossip*, 29 P.3d at 603.

5. *Warner v. Gross*, No. CIV-14-0665-F, 2014 WL 7671680 (W.D. Okla., Dec. 2014).

6. *Warner v. Gross*, 135 S. Ct. 824 (2015) (Sotomayor, J., dissenting).

7. *Id.*

8. *Id.*

9. M. Delatorre, Ed Doney, & Abby Broyles, Oklahoma Inmate Said His "Body Was on Fire" Prior to Being Executed for 1997 Murder and Rape, KFOR.com, Jan. 15, 2015, at http://kfor.com/2015/01/15 /oklahoma-inmate-said-his-body-was-on-fire-prior-to-be-executed-for -1997-murder-and-rape; Nolan Clay & Rick Green, Wrong Drug Used for January Execution, State Records Show, The Oklahoman, Oct. 8, 2015, at http://newsok.com/wrong-drug-used-for-january-execution-state -records-show/article/5452084.

10. *Glossip v. Gross*, 135 S. Ct. 2726, 2733 (2015).

11. James Gibson & Corinna Barrett Lain, *Death Penalty Drugs and the International Moral Marketplace*, 103 Georgetown L.J. 1215, 1242 (2015).

12. European Commission, Press Release Database, *Commission Extends Control over Goods Which Could Be Used for Capital Punishment or Torture* (Brussels, Dec. 20, 2011), at http://europa.eu/rapid /press-release_IP-11-1578_en.htm.

13. Protocol No. 6 to the Convention for the Protection of Human Rights and Fundamental Freedoms Concerning the Abolition of the Death Penalty, ETS 114 (Apr. 28, 1983; entered into force Mar. 1, 1985), Art. 1; Protocol No. 13 to the Convention for the Protection of Human Rights and Fundamental Freedoms Concerning the Abolition of the Death Penalty in All Circumstances, ETS 187 (May 3, 2002; entered into force July 1, 2003), Art. 1.

14. Andrew Drilling, *Capital Punishment: The Global Trend Toward Abolition and Its Implications for the United States*, 40 Ohio N.U. L. Rev. 847, 865 (2014).

15. Linda Greenhouse, *Becoming Justice Blackmun: Harry Blackmun's Supreme Court Journey* (New York: Times Books, 2005), p. 167.

16. *Warner*, 135 S. Ct. at 826–27 (Sotomayor, J., dissenting).

17. Cary Aspinwall, Charles Warner Is Executed, Tulsa World, Jan. 14, 2015, at www.tulsaworld.com/news/courts/charles-warner-is -executed-here-s-the-story-of-his/article_af39c542-08d0-5bd6-80ac -01a6f1c668ee.html; Cary Aspinwall & Ziva Branstetter, Oklahoma Executes Charles Warner in 20-minute Procedure; State Says No Complications, Tulsa World, Jan. 16, 2015, at www.tulsaworld.com/news homepage1/oklahoma-executes-charles-warner-in--minute-procedure -state-says/article_134dd8b3-0024-574e-a732-f3b466274f1c.html; Dana Ford, Oklahoma Executes Charles Warner, CNN, Jan. 16, 2015, at www.cnn.com/2015/01/15/us/oklahoma-execution-charles-frederick -warner.

18. John F. Stinneford, *Death, Desuetude, and Original Meaning*, 56 Wm. & Mary L. Rev. 531, 539–40 (2014) ("Justice Antonin Scalia is the most prominent advocate of the position that, absent constitutional amendment, the death penalty can never be declared unconstitutional consistent with the original meaning of the Cruel and Unusual Punishments Clause."); *id.* at 542 ("Justice Scalia appears to believe that the Cruel and Unusual Punishments Clause is a positive legal norm that forbids only those punishments that violate the standards of cruelty that prevailed in 1791."); Steven G. Gey, *Justice Scalia's Death Penalty*, 20 Fla. St. U. L. Rev. 67, 129 (1992) ("Scalia's basic principle is simply that 'the People' are permitted to decide 'what is a crime and what constitutes aggravation and mitigation of a crime.' In other words, if 'the People' want to use the death penalty, then no further utilitarian proof, support, or justification is necessary.") (quoting *Payne v. Tennessee*, 111 S. Ct. 2597, 2613 (1991) (Scalia, J., concurring)).

19. Transcript of Oral Argument (Apr. 29, 2015), *Glossip v. Gross*, *supra* note 1, at pp. 3–20; Austin Sarat, The Trouble with Oklahoma's New Execution Technique, Politico Magazine, Apr. 20, 2015, at www .politico.com/magazine/story/2015/04/oklahoma-death-penalty-gas -chamber-117156.

20. *In re Kemmler*, 136 U.S. 436, 446 (1890); *Wilkerson v. Utah*, 99 U.S. 130, 134–36 (1879); *see also Weems v. United States*, 217 U.S. 349, 404 (1910) (White, J., dissenting) ("So long as they do not provide cruel and unusual punishments, such as disgraced the civilization of

former ages, and made one shudder with horror to read of them, as drawing, quartering, burning, etc., the Constitution does not put any limit upon legislative discretion."); *Glass v. Louisiana*, 471 U.S. 1080, 1084 (1985) (Brennan, J., dissenting from denial of cert.) ("in explaining the obvious unconstitutionality of such ancient practices as disemboweling while alive, drawing and quartering, public dissection, burning alive at the stake, crucifixion, and breaking at the wheel, the Court has emphasized that the Eighth Amendment forbids 'inhuman and barbarous' methods of execution that go at all beyond 'the mere extinguishment of life' and cause 'torture or a lingering death' ") (citing *In re Kemmler*, 136 U.S. at 447); *Baze v. Rees*, 553 U.S. 35, 101 (2008) (Thomas, J., dissenting) ("It strains credulity to suggest that the defining characteristic of burning at the stake, disemboweling, drawing and quartering, beheading, and the like was that they involved risks of pain that could be eliminated by using alternative methods of execution. Quite plainly, what defined these punishments was that they were *designed* to inflict torture as a way of enhancing a death sentence; they were *intended* to produce a penalty worse than death, to accomplish something 'more than the mere extinguishment of life.' ") (emphasis in original).

21. Mark Sherman, Supreme Court Upholds Use of Controversial Execution Drug, Philly.com, June 30, 2015, at www.philly.com/philly/news/nation_world/20150630_Supreme_Court_upholds_use_of_controversial_execution_drug.html.

22. Dahlia Lithwick, Supreme Court Breakfast Table: Scalia Goes Off Script, Slate, June 29, 2015, at www.slate.com/articles/news_and_politics/the_breakfast_table/features/2015/scotus_roundup/scalia_in_glossip_v_gross_supreme_court_decision_oklahoma_may_kill_using.html.

23. Ariane de Vogue, Supreme Court Backs Use of Lethal Injection Drug, CNN, June 29, 2015, at http://www.cnn.com/2015/06/29/politics/supreme-court-lethal-injection-ruling/.

24. Linda Hirshman, *Sisters in Law: How Sandra Day O'Connor and Ruth Bader Ginsburg Went to the Supreme Court and Changed the World* (New York: HarperCollins, 2015).

25. *Glossip*, 135 S. Ct. at 2730–31.

26. Clare Cushman, ed., *The Supreme Court Justices: Illustrated Biographies, 1789–2012* (Thousand Oaks, CA: CQ Press, 3d ed. 2013), pp. 505, 513.

27. 42 U.S.C. § 1983.

28. Goodwin Liu & Lynsay Skiba, Judge Alito and the Death Penalty, American Constitution Society for Law and Policy (Dec. 2005), p. 1.

29. *Glossip,* 135 S. Ct. at 2731.

30. *Baze v. Rees,* 553 U.S. 35, 69 (2008) (Alito, J., concurring) ("[p]ublic policy on the death penalty, an issue that stirs deep emotions, cannot be dictated by the testimony of an expert or two or by judicial findings of fact based on such testimony").

31. *Glossip,* 135 S. Ct. at 2731.

32. *Wilkerson v. Utah,* 99 U.S. 130, 134–35 (1879).

33. *In re Kemmler,* 136 U.S. 436, 444–49 (1890).

34. *Louisiana ex rel. Francis v. Resweber,* 329 U.S. 459, 463–64 (1947) (plurality opinion).

35. *Baze v. Rees,* 553 U.S. 35, 61 (2008) (plurality opinion).

36. *Glossip,* 135 S. Ct. at 2732.

37. *Id.* at 2739.

38. *Id.* at 2734–35.

39. *Id.* at 2736.

40. *Id.* at 2782–83 (Sotomayor, J., dissenting).

41. *Id.* at 2739.

42. *Id.* at 2737–38.

43. *Id.* at 2738.

44. *Id.* at 2733.

45. *Id.* at 2745.

46. *Id.* at 2746 (quoting *id.* at 2795 (Sotomayor, J., dissenting)).

47. *Id.* at 2746 (Scalia, J., concurring).

48. *Id.* at 2747 (Scalia, J., concurring).

49. *Ford v. Wainwright,* 477 U.S. 399 (1986).

50. *Atkins v. Virginia,* 536 U.S. 304 (2002); *Hall v. Florida,* 134 S. Ct. 1986 (2014).

51. *Roper v. Simmons,* 543 U.S. 551 (2005).

52. *Coker v. Georgia,* 433 U.S. 584 (1977); *Enmund v. Florida,* 458 U.S. 782 (1982); *Kennedy v. Louisiana,* 554 U.S. 407 (2008). *But*

cf. *Tison v. Arizona,* 481 U.S. 137 (1987) (allowing the death penalty for a felony murderer who was a major participant in the underlying felony and exhibited a reckless indifference to human life).

53. *E.g., Gregg v. Georgia,* 428 U.S. 153 (1976).

54. *E.g., Baze,* 553 U.S. at 87–88 (Scalia, J., concurring).

55. Antonin Scalia, California Lawyer (Jan. 2011).

56. John D. Bessler, *Cruel and Unusual: The American Death Penalty and the Founders' Eighth Amendment* (Boston: Northeastern University Press, 2012), p. 26.

57. Scalia Talks Death Penalty at University of Minnesota Law School, CBS Minnesota, Oct. 20, 2015, at http://minnesota.cbslocal .com/2015/10/20/scalia-talks-death-penalty-at-university-of -minnesota-law-school.

58. *Baze,* 553 U.S. at 87–88 (Scalia, J., concurring).

59. *Atkins v. Virginia,* 536 U.S. 304, 349 (2002) (Scalia, J, dissenting).

60. John D. Bessler, *The Death Penalty in Decline: From Colonial America to the Present,* 50 Crim. L. Bull. 245, 261 (2014). The United States also moved away from public executions from the 1830s to the 1930s, with states also experimenting with nighttime executions beginning in the nineteenth century. One minute after midnight became a popular time to conduct executions, with more than 80% of U.S. executions taking place from 1977 to 1995 occurring between 11:00 p.m. and 7:30 a.m. More than 50% of those 313 executions took place between midnight and 1:00 a.m. John D. Bessler, *Death in the Dark: Midnight Executions in America* (Boston: Northeastern University Press, 1997), p. 81.

61. Bessler, *Cruel and Unusual,* pp. 215, 268, 314.

62. *Id.* at 326–27; Randy E. Barnett, *Scalia's Infidelity: A Critique of "Faint-Hearted" Originalism,* 75 U. Cin. L. Rev. 7, 12–13 (2006) (quoting Antonin Scalia, *Originalism: The Lesser Evil,* 57 U. Cin. L. Rev. 849, 864 (1989)).

63. Jennifer Senior, In Conversation: Antonin Scalia, New York, Oct. 6, 2013, at http://nymag.com/news/features/antonin-scalia-2013-10/.

64. *Glossip,* 135 S. Ct. at 2747 (Scalia, J., concurring) (quoting *id.* at 2781 (Breyer, J., dissenting)).

65. *Id.* at 2747 (Scalia, J., concurring).

66. Megan Spicer, Speaking at Yale, Justice Breyer Calls Scalia "Titan of Law," The Connecticut Law Tribune, Feb. 17, 2016, at www .ctlawtribune.com/id=1202749971104/Speaking-at-Yale-Justice -Breyer-Calls-Scalia-Titan-of-Law?slreturn=20160118213651.

67. *Glossip*, 135 S. Ct. at 2747–48 (Scalia, J., concurring).

68. *Id*. at 2749 (Scalia, J., concurring).

69. Michael Johnson, *Fifteen Years and Death: Double Jeopardy, Multiple Punishments, and Extended Stays on Death Row*, 23 B.U. Pub. Int. L.J. 85, 86–90 (2014); Time on Death Row, Death Penalty Information Center, at www.deathpenaltyinfo.org/time-death-row.

70. *Glossip*, 135 S. Ct. at 2769 (Breyer, J., dissenting).

71. *Id*. at 2748 (Scalia, J., concurring).

72. *Id*. (Scalia, J., concurring).

73. *Id*. at 2749 (Scalia, J., concurring).

74. *Id*. (Scalia, J., concurring) (citing *id*. at 2764–65 (Breyer, J., dissenting)).

75. *Id*. (Scalia, J., concurring) (quoting *Trop v. Dulles*, 356 U.S. 86, 101 (1958)).

76. *Id*. (Scalia, J., concurring).

77. *Smith v. Arizona*, 552 U.S. 985 (2007) (Breyer, J., dissenting); *Lackey v. Texas*, 514 U.S. 1045 (1995) (memo. of Justice Stevens respecting the denial of cert.) (quoting *Riley v. Attorney General of Jamaica* [1983] 1 A.C. 719, 734, 3 All E.R. 469, 478 (P.C. 1983) (Lord Scarman, dissenting, joined by Lord Brightman)).

78. John D. Bessler, *The Birth of American Law: An Italian Philosopher and the American Revolution* (Durham, NC: Carolina Academic Press, 2014); Office of the High Commissioner, *Moving Away from the Death Penalty: Arguments, Trends and Perspectives* (New York: United Nations, 2014).

79. *McGautha v. California*, 402 U.S. 183, 196 (1971).

80. *Furman v. Georgia*, 408 U.S. 238 (1972).

81. *Gregg v. Georgia*, 428 U.S. 153 (1976); *Proffitt v. Florida*, 428 U.S. 242 (1976); *Jurek v. Texas*, 428 U.S. 262 (1976).

82. *Gregg*, 428 U.S. at 168.

83. *Glossip*, 135 S. Ct. at 2749 (Scalia, J., concurring). In addition to executions becoming unusual in most American states, they have

also become highly unusual at the federal level, in the U.S. military, and in most nations (if they are used at all). *See, e.g.,* Rich Federico, *The Unusual Punishment: A Call for Congress to Abolish the Death Penalty Under the Uniform Code of Military Justice for Unique Military, Non-Homicide Offenses,* 18 BERKELEY J. CRIM. L. 1, 16–25 (2013); *State v. Santiago,* 122 A.3d 1, 10 (Conn. 2015) ("the death penalty now constitutes cruel and unusual punishment, in violation of the state constitution"); *see also United States v. Sampson,* Cr. No. 01-10384-MLW, 2015 WL 7962394 *12 ("When viewed in the context of the world as a whole, the death penalty has become unusual.").

84. *Glossip,* 135 S. Ct. at 2749 (Scalia, J., concurring).

85. *Trop v. Dulles,* 356 U.S. 86, 101 (1958).

86. *Glossip,* 135 S. Ct. at 2749–50 (Scalia, J., concurring). During the Enlightenment, many of America's founders *embraced* the writings of the Italian philosopher and criminal law-theorist Cesare Beccaria, a prominent anti–death penalty advocate. While they may not have gone as far as Beccaria suggested, they regularly concurred with many of the core or foundational principles he articulated—*proportionality* between crimes and punishments, that *certainty* is better than *severity* as far as punishment is concerned, and that any punishment that goes beyond *absolute necessity* is tyrannical. Bessler, *The Birth of American Law,* p. 653 (containing index entries for "proportionality" and "punishment(s)," citing various pages where these principles are discussed in greater detail). At the time of the 1787 Constitutional Convention in Philadelphia, it must be remembered, there was no American penitentiary system. Beccaria's then novel ideas were seen as ones that needed to be tested, with James Madison viewing Beccaria as a "Philosophical Legislator." 9 Gaillard Hunt, ed., *The Writings of James Madison* (New York: G. P. Putnam's Sons, 1910), p. 300.

87. *Roper v. Simmons,* 543 U.S. 551, 607 (2005) (Scalia, J., dissenting; joined by Chief Justice Rehnquist and Justice Thomas); *Atkins v. Virginia,* 536 U.S. 304, 337 (2002) (Scalia, J., dissenting; joined by Chief Justice Rehnquist and Justice Thomas).

88. *Glossip,* 135 S. Ct. at 2750 & n.1 (Thomas, J., concurring) (citations omitted).

89. *Id.* at 2750–51 (Thomas, J., concurring) (quoting *Harmelin v. Michigan,* 501 U.S. 957, 966 (1991) (opinion of Scalia, J.)).

90. *Id.* at 2751–52 (Thomas, J., concurring).

91. *Id.* at 2752–55 (Thomas, J., concurring).

92. *Id.* at 2780–81 (Sotomayor, J., dissenting).

93. *Id.* at 2781 (Sotomayor, J., dissenting).

94. *Id.* at 2782 (Sotomayor, J., dissenting).

95. *Id.* at 2783 (Sotomayor, J., dissenting).

96. *Id.* at 2785–86 (Sotomayor, J., dissenting).

97. *Id.* at 2789 (Sotomayor, J., dissenting).

98. *Id.* at 2781 (Sotomayor, J., dissenting).

99. *Id.* at 2755 (Breyer, J., dissenting).

100. *Id.* at 2776–77 (Breyer, J., dissenting).

101. *Id.* at 2755–56 (Breyer, J., dissenting).

102. Kenneth Jost, ed., *The Supreme Court A to Z* (New York: Routledge, 2d ed. 2013), p. 96; Joan Biskupic & Elder Witt, *The Supreme Court at Work* (Washington, DC: Congressional Quarterly, 1997), p. 240.

103. *E.g.*, Stephen Breyer, *Active Liberty: Interpreting Our Democratic Constitution* (New York: Vintage Books, 2005); Stephen Breyer, *The Court and the World: American Law and the New Global Realities* (New York: Alfred A. Knopf, 2015); *see also* Robert Badinter & Stephen Breyer, eds., *Judges in Contemporary Democracy: An International Conversation* (New York: New York University Press, 2004). Notably, Justice Breyer's coeditor on the latter book is Robert Badinter, a French lawyer who served as the Minister of Justice under French president François Mitterrand. Born in 1928, Badinter represented Roger Bontems, a convict serving a 20-year sentence for robbery who, along with a fellow prisoner, Claude Buffet, took a prison guard and a nurse hostage in the prison infirmary during a 1971 revolt at Clairvaux Prison. When the police stormed the building, Buffet—then serving a life sentence for murder—slit the throats of the hostages. At the trial of Buffet and Bontems, hundreds of people gathered outside the courthouse and chanted, "*À Mort! À Mort!*" ("To death, to death"). Both men were, in fact, sentenced to death, although Buffet was the one who killed both hostages. Badinter served as the French Minister of Justice from 1981 to 1986, then became the President of the Constitutional Council of France from 1986 to 1995. Badinter—of particular note here—successfully advocated for the death penalty's abolition in

France in 1981. After representing Bontems and witnessing his client be guillotined in Paris in 1972, Badinter vowed to campaign against the death penalty. Badinter has committed much of his life to that cause. *See* Robert Badinter, *Abolition: One Man's Battle Against the Death Penalty* (Boston: Northeastern University Press, Jeremy Mercer, trans. 2008); Jeremy Mercer, *When the Guillotine Fell: The Bloody Beginning and Horrifying End to France's River of Blood, 1791–1977* (New York: St. Martin's Press, 2008), pp. 180–82, 281–83; Robert Frederick Opie, *Guillotine* (Stroud, Gloucestershire: The History Press, 2013), ch. 1.

104. Melvin I. Urofsky, ed., *Biographical Encyclopedia of the Supreme Court: The Lives and Legal Philosophies of the Justices* (Washington, DC: CQ Press, 2006), pp. 74–75; Clare Cushman, ed., *The Supreme Court Justices: Illustrated Biographies, 1789–2012* (Thousand Oaks, CA: CQ Press, 3d ed. 2013), p. 493.

105. *Brown v. Board of Education,* 347 U.S. 483 (1954); *Gideon v. Wainwright,* 372 U.S. 335 (1963); *Griswold v. Connecticut,* 381 U.S. 479 (1965); *Miranda v. Arizona,* 384 U.S. 436 (1966).

106. Stephen G. Breyer, Preface to *The Jewish Justices of the Supreme Court Revisited: Brandeis to Fortas* (Washington, DC: The Supreme Court Historical Society, Jennifer M. Lowe ed., 1994), p. 1.

107. David Feith, ed., *Teaching America: The Case for Civic Education* (Lanham, MD: Rowman & Littlefield, 2011), p. 27; Rebecca Stefoff, *Furman v. Georgia: Debating the Death Penalty* (New York: Marshall Cavendish, 2007), pp. 64–65.

108. Peter Hodgkinson & Andrew Rutherford, eds., *Capital Punishment: Global Issues and Prospects* (Winchester, UK: Waterside Press, 1996), p. 266.

109. *Hudson v. McMillian,* 503 U.S. 1, 9 (1992); *Wilkerson,* 99 U.S. at 136.

110. Simone Payment, *The Trial of Leopold and Loeb: A Primary Source Account* (New York: The Rosen Publishing Group, 2004), p. 6; John A. Farrell, *Clarence Darrow: Attorney for the Damned* (New York: Vintage Books, 2012), pp. 333–35, 357; Troy Taylor, *True Crime, Illinois: The State's Most Notorious Criminal Cases* (Mechanicsburg, PA: Stackpole Books, 2009), pp. 34–41; Eliezer J. Sternberg, *My Brain*

Made Me Do It: The Rise of Neuroscience and the Threat to Moral Responsibility (Amherst, NY: Prometheus Books, 2010), pp. 121–22; Evan J. Mandery, *A Wild Justice: The Death and Resurrection of Capital Punishment in America* (New York: W.W. Norton & Co., 2013), p. 6.

111. Hodgkinson & Rutherford, eds., *Capital Punishment*, p. 266; *see also* Herbert H. Haines, *Against Capital Punishment: The Anti-Death Penalty Movement in America, 1972–1994* (New York: Oxford University Press, 1996), p. 26 ("Justice Goldberg's reservations about capital punishment were not the results of a sudden revelation. In a 1973 speech, he stated that his doubts had been growing since his days as a lawyer, well before his appointment to the Supreme Court.").

112. Arthur J. Goldberg, *Death and the Supreme Court*, 15 HAST. CONST. L.Q. 1 (1987); *see also* Arthur J. Goldberg, The Death Penalty and the Supreme Court, The Christian Science Monitor, Aug. 25, 1987.

113. Laura Kay, *The Legacy of a Supreme Court Clerkship: Stephen Breyer and Arthur Goldberg*, 115 PENN. ST. L. REV. 83, 100 (2010).

114. Bernard Schwartz, *The Unpublished Opinions of the Warren Court* (Oxford: Oxford University Press, 1985), pp. 396, 407.

115. *Id.* at 395, 401.

116. Arthur J. Goldberg, *Death and the Supreme Court*, 15 HASTINGS CONST. L. Q. 1, 1–2 (1987); Arthur J. Goldberg, *Memorandum to the Conference Re: Capital Punishment, October Term, 1963*, 27 S. TEX. L. REV. 493 (1986); *see also Rudolph v. Alabama,* 375 U.S. 889 (1963) (Goldberg, J., dissenting; joined by Douglas & Brennan, JJ.).

117. U.S. CONST., amend. VIII; *Roper v. Simmons,* 543 U.S. 551, 577 (2005); *Harmelin v. Michigan,* 501 U.S. 957, 966 (1991); Bessler, *Cruel and Unusual*, pp. 94, 155, 178. Early American state constitutions commonly prohibited "cruel and unusual," "cruel or unusual," or simply "cruel" punishments. *Id.* at 177–80. But the U.S. Constitution's Eighth Amendment—as originally interpreted—only constrained the *federal* government. *Barron v. Baltimore,* 32 U.S. (7 Pet.) 243, 250 (1833).

118. *See generally* Steve Pincus, *1688: The First Modern Revolution* (New Haven: Yale University Press, 2009).

119. Alvin Rabushka, *Taxation in Colonial America* (Princeton, NJ: Princeton University Press, 2008), p. 280.

120. VA. DECLARATION OF RIGHTS, § IX (June 12, 1776); Lyon Gardiner Tyler, *Williamsburg, the Old Colonial Capital* (Richmond, VA: Whittet & Shepperson, 1907), p. 212.

121. 2 Ralph A. Rossum & G. Alan Tarr, *American Constitutional Law: The Bill of Rights and Subsequent Amendments* (Boulder, CO: Westview Press, 9th ed., 2014), p. 52; Akhil Reed Amar, *The Bill of Rights and the Fourteenth Amendment*, 101 Yale L.J. 1193, 1219–20 (1992).

122. U.S. CONST., amend. XIV.

123. Akhil Reed Amar, *America's Constitution: A Biography* (New York: Random House, 2006), pp. 387–88; Garrett Epps, *Democracy Reborn: The Fourteenth Amendment and the Fight for Equal Rights in Post–Civil War America* (New York: Henry Holt and Co., 2006), pp. 167–71.

124. *Robinson v. California*, 370 U.S. 660, 660–67 (1962).

125. *See* John D. Bessler, *The Anomaly of Executions: The Cruel and Unusual Punishments Clause in the 21st Century*, 2 BRIT. J. AM. LEGAL STUDIES 297 (2013); *Farmer v. Brennan*, 511 U.S. 825, 828, 832 (1994); *Hope v. Pelzer*, 536 U.S. 730, 733–34, 738 (2002); *Estelle v. Gamble*, 429 U.S. 97, 102–103 (1976); *Hutto v. Finney*, 437 U.S. 678, 685 (1978); *Rhodes v. Chapman*, 452 U.S. 337, 346 (1981); *Hudson v. McMillian*, 503 U.S. 1, 4–9 (1992); *Helling v. McKinney*, 509 U.S. 25, 33–35 (1993); *Brown v. Plata*, 131 S. Ct. 1910, 1928–29 (2011); *Jackson v. Bishop*, 404 F.2d 571, 579–80 (8th Cir. 1968) (Blackmun, J.).

126. Dara Lind, The Supreme Court's Big Death-Penalty Fight Just Exploded into the Open, Vox, June 29, 2015, at www.vox.com/2015/6/29/8862805/death-penalty-supreme-court-breyer.

127. *Statements on the Death Penalty by Supreme Court Justices,* Death Penalty Information Center, at http://www.deathpenaltyinfo.org/statements-death-penalty-supreme-court-justices.

128. U.S. CONST., amend. VIII.

129. *See generally* Michael Mello, *Against the Death Penalty: The Relentless Dissents of Justices Brennan and Marshall* (Boston: Northeastern University Press, 1996).

130. Bessler, *The Anomaly of Executions*, pp. 308–309.

131. *Kansas v. Marsh,* 548 U.S. 163, 207 (2006) (Souter, J., dissenting; joined by Stevens, Ginsburg & Breyer, JJ.).

132. *Baze v. Rees*, 553 U.S. 35, 113 (2008) (Breyer, J., concurring).

133. *Medellín v. Texas,* 552 U.S. 491, 496–99 (2008); *id.* at 538, 563 (Breyer, J., dissenting).

134. Allan Turner & Rosanna Ruiz, Medellin Executed for Rape, Murder of Houston Teens, Houston Chronicle, Aug. 5, 2008, at www.chron.com/news/houston-texas/article/Medellin-executed-for-rape-murder-of-Houston-1770696.php.

135. *Leal Garcia v. Texas,* 131 S. Ct. 2866, 2869, 2871 (2011) (Breyer, J., dissenting).

136. Chris McGreal, Humberto Leal Garcia Executed in Texas Despite White House Appeal, The Guardian, July 7, 2011, at www.theguardian.com/world/2011/jul/08/humberto-leal-garcia-executed-texas.

137. *Uttecht v. Brown,* 551 U.S. 1, 4, 10 (2007); *id.* at 35, 44 (Stevens, J., dissenting; joined by Souter, Ginsburg, and Breyer, JJ.) (quoting *Wainwright v. Witt,* 469 U.S. 412, 420 (1985)); *see also id.* at 44 (Breyer, J., dissenting; joined by Justice Souter).

138. *E.g., Justice Stevens (Retired) on the Death Penalty,* Death Penalty Information Center, at www.deathpenaltyinfo.org/statements-death-penalty-supreme-court-justices#stevens.

139. Tom Goldstein, What Happens to This Term's Close Cases?, SCOTUSblog, Feb. 13, 2016, at www.scotusblog.com/2016/02/what-happens-to-this-terms-close-cases/ (noting that if the U.S. Supreme Court Justices are divided four-to-four, "there is no majority for a decision and the lower court's ruling stands, as if the Supreme Court had never heard the case").

140. Antonin Scalia & Bryan Garner, *Making Your Case: The Art of Persuading Judges* (St. Paul, MN: Thomson/West, 2008); Antonin Scalia & Bryan Garner, *Reading Law: The Interpretation of Legal Texts* (St. Paul, MN: Thomson/West, 2012).

141. Bryan A. Garner, Textual Citations Make Legal Writing Onerous, for Lawyers and Nonlawyers Alike, ABA Journal, Feb. 1, 2014, at www.abajournal.com/magazine/article/textual_citations_make_legal_writing_onerous_for_lawyers_and_nonlawyers.

142. James A. McCafferty, ed., *Capital Punishment* (New Brunswick, NJ: AldineTransaction, 2010), p. 198; Jeffrey L. Kirchmeier, *Imprisoned by the Past: Warren McCleskey and the American Death Penalty* (Oxford: Oxford University Press, 2015), p. 75. In 1966, Evans received a posthumous pardon. Saundra D. Westervelt & John A. Humphrey, ed., *Wrongfully Convicted: Perspectives on Failed Justice* (New Brunswick, NJ: Rutgers University Press, 2005), p. 273.

143. Steven Wilf, *Law's Imagined Republic: Popular Politics and Criminal Justice in Revolutionary America* (Cambridge: Cambridge University Press, 2010), p. 139; Randall Coyne & Lyn Entzeroth, *Capital Punishment and the Judicial Process* (Durham, NC: Carolina Academic Press, 4th ed. 2012), p. 4.

144. Scott Vollum, Rolando V. Del Carmen, Durant Frantzen, Claudia San Miguel, & Kelly Cheeseman, *The Death Penalty: Constitutional Issues, Commentaries, and Case Briefs* (New York: Routledge, 3d ed., 2005); p. 2; Juliet Haines Mofford, *"The Devil Made Me Do It!": Crime and Punishment in Early New England* (Guilford, CT: Globe Pequot Press, 2012), p. 5.

145. John D. Bessler, *The Death Penalty in Decline: From Colonial America to the Present*, 50 CRIM. L. BULL. 245, 245 (2014).

146. Stuart Banner, *The Death Penalty: An American History* (Cambridge, MA: Harvard University Press, 2002), pp. 74–75, 214; 4 Joseph Chitty, *A Practical Treatise on the Criminal Law* (London: Samuel Brooke, 2d ed. 1826), p. 366; Gabriele Gottlieb, Theater of Death: Capital Punishment in Early America, 1750–1800, Ph. D. thesis, University of Pittsburgh (2005), pp. 29, 81 129, 229.

147. Bessler, *The Death Penalty in Decline*, pp. 245–26.

148. Frederick Rosen, *Classical Utilitarianism from Hume to Mill* (New York: Routledge, 2003), pp. 145–46.

149. Bessler, *Cruel and Unusual*, p. 37.

150. Bessler, *The Birth of American Law*, p. 4; William A. Schabas, *The Abolition of the Death Penalty in International Law* (Cambridge: Cambridge University Press, 3d ed. 2002), p. 5.

151. *See generally* Bessler, *Cruel and Unusual*, pp. 31–58; Bessler, *The Birth of American Law*, ch. 3.

152. Banner, *The Death Penalty*, p. 91; Louis Masur, *Rites of Execution: Capital Punishment and the Transformation of American Culture, 1776–1865* (Oxford: Oxford University Press, 1989), p. 175 n.10.

153. John D. Bessler, *Revisiting Beccaria's Vision: The Enlightenment, America's Death Penalty, and the Abolition Movement*, 4 Nw. J.L. & Soc. Pol'y 195, 207–08 (2009); John Adams Diary, June 28, 1770, available at Massachusetts Historical Society, Adams Family Papers, an Electronic Archive.

154. *The North American Review* (Boston: Charles C. Little & James Brown, 1850), Vol. 71, p. 440 (reprinting 2 Charles Francis Adams, *The Works of John Adams, Second President of the United States: With a Life of the Author, Notes, and Illustrations* (Boston: Charles C. Little & James Brown, 1850)).

155. Robin Healey, *Italian Literature Before 1900 in English Translation: An Annotated Bibliography* (Toronto: University of Toronto Press, 2011), p. 253; Aaron Thomas, ed., Aaron Thomas & Jeremy Parzen, trans., Cesare Beccaria, *On Crimes and Punishments and Other Writings* (Toronto: University of Toronto Press, 2008), pp. 17, 26, 32–34, 51, 55–56.

156. Bessler, *Cruel and Unusual*, pp. 51–53.

157. *Id.* at 48–49.

158. *Id.* at 48.

159. Kent S. Miller & Michael L. Radelet, *Executing the Mentally Ill: The Criminal Justice System and the Case of Alvin Ford* (Newbury Park, CA: Sage Publications, 1993), p. 111 n.5; John Ferling, *Adams vs. Jefferson: The Tumultuous Election of 1800* (Oxford: Oxford University Press, 2004), pp. xi–xii.

160. Bessler, *Cruel and Unusual*, pp. 86–87, 108.

161. *Id.* at 49.

162. *Id.* at 178.

163. *Id.* at 179–81.

164. *Id.* at 54; Bessler, *The Birth of American Law*, pp. 182–83.

165. Antonio Pace, ed., *Luigi Castiglioni's Viaggio: Travels in the United States of North America 1785–1787* (Syracuse, NY: Syracuse University Press, 1983), pp. 313–14.

166. *Id.* at xii, xxix–xxxiv.

167. *Id.* at 313–14.

168. Cornell W. Clayton, *The Politics of Justice: The Attorney General and the Making of Legal Policy* (New York: Routledge, 2015), pp. xv, 17; Robert A. Nowlan, *The American Presidents, Washington to Tyler: What They Did, What They Said, What Was Said About Them, with Full Source Notes* (Jefferson, NC: McFarland & Co., 2012), p. 165; James McMurtry Longo, *From Classroom to White House: The Presidents and First Ladies as Students and Teachers* (Jefferson, NC: McFarland & Co., 2012), p. 23.

169. Pace, ed., *Luigi Castiglioni's Viaggio*, pp. 313–14.

170. Bessler, *The Birth of American Law*, pp. 303–6.

171. Pace, ed., *Luigi Castiglioni's Viaggio*, p. 314.

172. *Id.*, pp. 1–269.

173. *Id.*, p. 314.

174. Akhil Reed Amar, *The Bill of Rights: Creation and Reconstruction* (New Haven, CT: Yale University Press, 1998), p. 87.

175. Bessler, *Cruel and Unusual*, pp. 94–95; Nicholas M. McLean, *Livelihood, Ability to Pay, and the Original Meaning of the Excessive Fines Clause*, 40 HAST. CONST. L. Q. 833, 858–59 (2013).

176. Bessler, *Cruel and Unusual*, pp. 174–76.

177. Philip Babcock Gove, ed., *Webster's Third New International Dictionary of the English Language Unabridged* (Springfield, MA: Merriam-Webster, 2002), p. 1716.

178. *See generally* Bessler, *The Birth of American Law.*

179. Lorenzo Sears, *John Hancock: The Picturesque Patriot* (Boston: Little, Brown, & Co., 1913), pp. 109, 228.

180. Brian Steele, *Thomas Jefferson and American Nationhood* (Cambridge: Cambridge University Press, 2012), p. 40 n.136.

181. Bessler, *Cruel and Unusual*, p. 47.

182. *See, e.g.*, Steve Coffman, comp. & ed., *Words of the Founding Fathers: Selected Quotations of Franklin, Washington, Adams, Jefferson, Madison and Hamilton, with Sources* (Jefferson, NC: McFarland & Co., 2012), pp. 8, 15, 69, 103, 106, 268, 277.

183. Bessler, *Cruel and Unusual*, p. 53.

184. Declaration of Independence (July 4, 1776).

185. Bessler, *The Birth of American Law*, pp. 186–87.

186. Bessler, *Cruel and Unusual*, pp. 54–55.

187. *Id.* at 141.

188. *Id.* at 130.

189. *Id.* at 130–31.

190. *Id.* at 157.

191. *Id.*

192. Lawrence M. Friedman, *A History of American Law* (New York: Simon & Schuster, 1985), p. 281.

193. Norval Morris & David J. Rothman, eds., *The Oxford History of the Prison: The Practice of Punishment in Western Society* (Oxford: Oxford University Press, 1995), p. 103; Douglas Bradburn, *The Citizenship Revolution: Politics & the Creation of the American Union 1774–1804* (Charlottesville: University of Virginia Press, 2009), p. 196.

194. Masur, *Rites of Execution*, p. 71.

195. Bessler, *Cruel and Unusual*, pp. 85–91 (italics in original).

196. Guyora Binder, *Felony Murder* (Stanford, CA: Stanford University Press, 2012), p. 128.

197. Mitchel P. Roth, *Prisons and Prison Systems: A Global Encyclopedia* (Westport, CT: Greenwood Press, 2006), p. 29.

198. Bessler, *Cruel and Unusual*, pp. 47–55.

199. Bessler, *Cruel and Unusual*, p. 52; 2 Maeva Marcus, ed., *The Documentary History of the Supreme Court of the United States, 1789–1800: The Justices on Circuit, 1790–1794* (New York: Columbia University Press, 1988), pp. 189–90, 402; Robert Aitken & Marilyn Aitken, *Law Makers, Law Breakers and Uncommon Trials* (Chicago, IL: American Bar Association, 2007), p. 15.

200. Rod Gragg, *Forged in Faith: How Faith Shaped the Birth of the Nation 1607–1776* (New York: Howard Books, 2010), pp. 22, 88, 185.

201. "A Bill for Proportioning Crimes and Punishments in Cases Heretofore Capital," *in* 2 Julian P. Boyd et al., eds., *The Papers of Thomas Jefferson* (Princeton, NJ: Princeton University Press, 1950).

202. Bessler, *Cruel and Unusual*, p. 142.

203. *Id.* at 141.

204. *Id.* at 145.

205. O. F. Lewis, *The Development of American Prisons and Prison Customs 1776–1845* (Albany, NY: Prison Association of New York, 1922), pp. 8–9, 11, 13–14, 46, 151, 257, 325, 342.

206. *Id.* at 25, 271, 293.

207. Mitchell P. Roth, *Prisons and Prison Systems: A Global Encyclopedia* (Westport, CT: Greenwood Press, 2006), p. 341.

208. Richard H. Phelps, *Newgate of Connecticut: A History of the Prison, Its Insurrections, Massacres, &c.* (Hartford, CT: Press of Elihu Geer, 3d ed. 1844), p. 4.

209. *United States v. Smith*, 18 U.S. 153, 157 (1820).

210. *Id.* at 164 (Livingston, J., dissenting); Daniel Allen Hearn, *Legal Executions in Delaware, the District of Columbia, Maryland, Virginia and West Virginia: A Comprehensive Registry, 1866–1962* (Jefferson, NC: McFarland & Co., 2015), p. 178; Joel H. Samuels, *The Full Story of* United States v. Smith, *America's Most Important Piracy Case*, 1 PENN. ST. J.L. & INT'L AFFAIRS 320, 347 n.124 & 356 (2012); *see also id.* at 347 n.124 ("On March 3, 1820, John Ferguson and Israel Denny, along with five others who had been aboard the *Irresistible*, were sentenced to death in Baltimore for their activities 'after a short but impressive address' by the sentencing judge. . . . Ferguson and Denny were executed on April 13, 1820, while the others were spared.").

211. *Ex parte* Wilson, 114 U.S. 417, 427 (1885).

212. *Id.* at 427–28. In its 1885 decision, the U.S. Supreme Court ruled, "Deciding nothing beyond what is required by the facts of the case before us, our judgment is that a crime punishable by imprisonment for a term of years at hard labor is an infamous crime, within the meaning of the fifth amendment of the constitution; and that the district court, in holding the petitioner to answer for such a crime, and sentencing him to such imprisonment, without indictment or presentment by a grand jury, exceeded its jurisdiction, and he is therefore entitled to be discharged." *Id.* at 429.

213. Bessler, *The Birth of American Law*, pp. 317–20.

214. Adam Lozeau, *Obscuring the Machinery of Death: Assessing the Constitutionality of Georgia's Lethal Injection Secrecy Law*, 32 LAW & INEQ. 451, 454 (2014).

215. *Id.* at 455; Bessler, *The Birth of American Law*, pp. 127, 209–10, 229.

216. William W. Berry III, *American Procedural Exceptionalism: A Deterrent or a Catalyst for Death Penalty Abolition?*, 17 CORNELL J.L. & PUB. POL'Y 481, 481–82 (2008); Alexis de Tocqueville, *Democracy in America*, Vol. 2 (Henry Reeve trans., 4th ed. 1840), pp. 176–77.

217. 3 *The Christian Examiner and Theological Review* (Boston: David Reed, 1826), pp. 204–5.

218. Harry Ammon, *James Monroe: The Quest for National Identity* (Charlottesville: University of Virginia Press, 1990), p. 180.

219. Shahid M. Shahidullah, *Crime Policy in America: Laws, Institutions, and Programs* (Lanham, MD: University Press of America, 2008), p. 61; Wilbur R. Miller, ed., *The Social History of Crime and Punishment in America: An Encyclopedia* (Thousand Oaks, CA: Sage Publications, 2012), p. 1074.

220. *James v. Commonwealth*, 1825 WL 1899 (Pa. 1825); Matthew W. Meskell, *The History of Prisons in the United States from 1777 to 1877*, 51 STAN. L. REV. 839, 841–42 (1999); 1 William Hawkins, *A Treatise of the Pleas of the Crown; or, A System of the Principal Matters Relating to that Subject, Digested Under Proper Heads* (London: Thomas Leach, ed., 6th ed. 1777), p. 624 (italics in original).

221. Bessler, *Cruel and Unusual*, p. 159.

222. G. F. H. Crockett, *An Address to the Legislature of Kentucky, on the Abolition of Capital Punishments, in the United States, and the Substitution of Exile for Life* (Georgetown, KY: N. L. Finnell, 1823).

223. Bessler, *Cruel and Unusual*, p. 158.

224. *Id.* at 159.

225. *Id.* at 196.

226. *Weems v. United States*, 217 U.S. 349, 357–58, 364–67, 381–82 (1910); Julian Go, Global Perspectives on the U.S. Colonial State in the Philippines, *in* Julian Go & Anne L. Foster, eds., *The American Colonial State in the Philippines: Global Perspectives* (Durham, NC: Duke University Press, 2003), p. 4.

227. *Trop v. Dulles*, 356 U.S. 86 (1958).

228. Nomination of Stephen G. Breyer to Be an Associate Justice of the Supreme Court of the United States, Hearings Before the Committee on the Judiciary, United States Senate, 103rd Cong., 2nd Sess. (July 12,

13, 14 & 15, 1994) (Washington, DC: U.S. Government Printing Office, 1995), pp. 137, 190–93, 233–37.

229. *Id.* at 236; Breyer Sworn In as High Court Justice in a Private Ceremony, L.A. Times, Aug. 4, 1994.

230. Jeffrey Toobin, *The Nine: Inside the Secret World of the Supreme Court* (New York: Doubleday, 2007); Jeffrey Toobin, Breyer's Big Idea: The Justice's Vision for a Progressive Revival on the Supreme Court, The New Yorker, Oct. 31, 2005.

231. Arthur J. Goldberg & Alan M. Dershowitz, *Declaring the Death Penalty Unconstitutional*, 83 HARV. L. REV. 1773 (1970); Alan M. Dershowitz, Justice Arthur Goldberg and His Law Clerks, *in* Todd C. Peppers and Artemus Ward, eds., *In Chambers: Stories of Supreme Court Law Clerks and Their Justices* (Charlottesville: University of Virginia Press, 2012), p. 295.

232. U.N. General Assembly, Universal Declaration of Human Rights (Dec. 10, 1948), 217 A(III).

233. *Haley v. Ohio,* 332 U.S. 592, 602 (1948) (Frankfurter, J., joining in reversal of judgment).

234. Banner, *The Death Penalty*, p. 239.

235. Melvin F. Wingersky, *Report of the Royal Commission on Capital Punishment (1949–1953): A Review*, 44 J. CRIM. L., CRIMINOLOGY, AND POLICE SCI. 695, 701 (1954).

236. Actually, Justice Harry Blackmun was *never* a believer in capital punishment, although he only articulated the view that the death penalty is unconstitutional as his retirement from the U.S. Supreme Court approached. In 1972, in dissenting in *Furman v. Georgia*, Blackmun "personally . . . rejoice[d]" at the U.S. Supreme Court's decision declaring the death penalty unconstitutional. As Blackmun wrote, "Cases such as these provide for me an excruciating agony of the spirit. I yield to no one in the depth of my distaste, antipathy, and, indeed, abhorrence, for the death penalty, with all its aspects of physical distress and fear and of moral judgment exercised by finite minds." Noting that his home state, Minnesota, had abolished the death penalty way back in 1911, he wrote, "That distaste is buttressed by a belief that capital punishment serves no useful purpose that can be demonstrated. For me, it violates childhood's training and life's experiences, and is not

compatible with the philosophical convictions I have been able to develop." Nonetheless, Blackmun—writing in the early 1970s as a member of the nation's highest court—found the Court's ruling in *Furman* "difficult to accept or to justify as a matter of history, of law, or of constitutional pronouncement." "I fear the Court has overstepped," he wrote. *Furman v. Georgia*, 408 U.S. 238, 405–406, 414 (1972) (Blackmun, J., dissenting). A botched hanging led to the abolition of the death penalty in Minnesota. *See* John D. Bessler, *Legacy of Violence: Lynch Mobs and Executions in Minnesota* (Minneapolis: University of Minnesota Press, 2003), ch. 6.

237. *Callins v. Collins,* 510 U.S. 1141, 1143, 1145 (1994) (Blackmun, J., dissenting).

238. Andrew Cohen, Now He Tells Us: John Paul Stevens Wants to Abolish the Death Penalty, The Atlantic, Apr. 7, 2014, at www.theatlantic.com/national/archive/2014/04/now-he-tells-us-john-paul-stevens-wants-to-abolish-the-death-penalty/359851; Justice Powell's New Wisdom, N.Y. Times, June 11, 1994, at www.nytimes.com/1994/06/11/opinion/justice-powell-s-new-wisdom.html.

239. Eliott C. McLaughlin, Oklahoma's Governor Stays Richard Glossip Execution, CNN, Oct. 1, 2015, at www.cnn.com/2015/09/30/us/oklahoma-richard-glossip-midazolam-execution.

240. "The Jury Never Heard It": Richard Glossip to Be Executed in Oklahoma Today Despite New Evidence, Democracy Now!, Sept. 30, 2015, at www.democracynow.org/2015/9/30/the_jury_never_heard _it_richard.

241. *Glossip v. State,* 157 P.3d 143, 164–65, 172–73 (2007) (Chapel, J., dissenting). Judge Arlene Johnson also dissented for the reasons set forth in Judge Chapel's dissenting opinion. Because the prosecution had "plastered" the courtroom with "poster-size trial notes taken by the prosecutor," Judge Johnson emphasized, the prosecution had, "in effect, a continuous closing argument, and may well have violated the rule of sequestration of witnesses." "This Court," she stressed, "cannot judge the effect of the process on this defendant's right to a fair trial with any assurance because the trial court refused the defendant's request to have the posters and their placement in the courtroom made part of the appellate record." *Id.* at 175 (Johnson, A., dissenting).

242. Leslie Rangel, Glossip's Attorneys: Documents Introduce New Evidence in Case, Could Prove Innocence, KFOR.com, Sept. 21, 2015, at http://kfor.com/2015/09/21/glossips-attorneys-documents -introduce-new-evidence-in-case-could-prove-innocence.

243. "The Jury Never Heard It": Richard Glossip to Be Executed in Oklahoma Today Despite New Evidence, Democracy Now!, Sept. 30, 2015, at www.democracynow.org/2015/9/30/the_jury_never_heard_it _richard.

244. Archbishop Carlo Maria Viganò to Gov. Mary Fallin (Sept. 19, 2015), at www.sisterhelen.org/wordpress/wp-content/uploads/Pope -letter-Glossip.png.

245. Eliott C. McLaughlin, Oklahoma's Governor Stays Richard Glossip Execution, CNN, Oct. 1, 2015, at www.cnn.com/2015/09/30 /us/oklahoma-richard-glossip-midazolam-execution.

246. *Glossip v. Oklahoma*, 136 S. Ct. 26 (2015); Eliott C. McLaughlin, Oklahoma's Governor Stays Richard Glossip Execution, CNN, Oct. 1, 2015, at www.cnn.com/2015/09/30/us/oklahoma-richard-glossip -midazolam-execution.

247. Dallas Franklin, Supreme Court Denies Stay, Glossip's Execution Moves Forward, KFOR.com, Sept. 30, 2015, at http://kfor.com /2015/09/30/glossips-attorneys-making-another-plea-during-11th-hour -for-stay-of-execution.

248. KFOR-TV & K. Querry, Gov. Mary Fallin Issues Stay of Execution for Richard Glossip Following Alleged Drug Mix-Up, KFOR .com, Sept. 30, 2015, at http://kfor.com/2015/09/30/gov-mary-fallin -issues-stay-of-execution-for-richard-glossip.

249. Eliott C. McLaughlin, Oklahoma's Governor Stays Richard Glossip Execution, CNN, Oct. 1, 2015, at www.cnn.com/2015/09/30 /us/oklahoma-richard-glossip-midazolam-execution.

250. Tracy Connor, "Oklahoma Governor Halts Richard Glossip Execution at Last Minute," NBC News, Sept. 30, 2015, at www.nbcnews .com/storyline/lethal-injection/pope-francis-tries-stop-richard-glossips -oklahoma-execution-n436166.

251. Oklahoma Is About to Execute an Innocent Man, Ministry Against the Death Penalty, at www.sisterhelen.org/richard/.

252. The Oklahoman Editorial Board, Getting Executions Right Is Focus for Oklahoma AG's Office, Feb. 3, 2016, at http://newsok.com

/article/5476357; Tracy Connor, "Oklahoma Governor Halts Richard Glossip Execution at Last Minute," NBC News, Sept. 30, 2015, at www.nbcnews.com/storyline/lethal-injection/pope-francis-tries-stop -richard-glossips-oklahoma-execution-n436166.

253. National Cooperative Highway Research Program, *Report 577: Guidelines for the Selection of Snow and Ice Control Materials to Mitigate Environmental Impacts* (Washington, DC: Transportation Research Board of the National Academies, 2007), p. 12; Matt Ford, An Oklahoma Execution Done Wrong, The Atlantic, Oct. 8, 2015, at www.theatlantic.com/politics/archive/2015/10/an-oklahoma-execution -done-wrong/409762.

254. Sean Murphy, Oklahoma Gov. Mary Fallin's General Counsel Has Resigned His Post Amid a Grand Jury Investigation Into How the Wrong Drug Was Delivered for Oklahoma's Last Two Scheduled Executions, The Republic (Columbus, IN), Feb. 11, 2016, at www .therepublic.com/view/story/3cea04e69ccc47b3982cded405e01249/US -Oklahoma-Execution-Resignation. On May 19, 2016, an Oklahoma grand jury issued a scathing, 106-page report detailing what Scott Pruitt, Oklahoma's attorney general, called a "careless, cavalier" attitude by those tasked with carrying out state executions. The grand jury itself found that "Department of Corrections staff, and others participating in the execution process, failed to perform their duties with the precision and attention to detail the exercise of state authority in such cases demands." Among its findings: (1) "the Director of the Department of Corrections . . . orally modified the execution protocol without authority"; (2) "the Pharmacist ordered the wrong execution drugs"; (3) "the Department's General Counsel failed to inventory the execution drugs as mandated by state purchasing requirements"; (4) the prison warden "failed to notify anyone in the Department that potassium acetate had been received"; (5) "the IV Team failed to observe the Department had received the wrong execution drugs"; and (6) "the Governor's General Counsel advocated the Department proceed with the Glossip execution using potassium acetate." In the words of an NBC News report: "The grand jury hammered Steve Mullins, who was then general counsel to Oklahoma Governor Mary Fallin, for advocating the state move ahead with the Glossip execution using the potassium acetate." When a prosecutor had objected, Mullins said potassium

chloride and potassium acetate were basically the same. "Google it," Mullins reportedly told the prosecutor. Mark Berman, Oklahoma Lethal Injection Process Muddled by 'Inexcusable Failure,' Grand Jury Finds, Washington Post, May 19, 2016, at www.washingtonpost.com /news/post-nation/wp/2016/05/19/oklahoma-grand-jury-says-lethal -injection-process-muddled-by-inexcusable-failure/; Tracy Connor, 'Careless and Cavalier': Grand Jury Issues Scathing Report on Botched Oklahoma Executions, NBC News, May 19, 2016, at www.nbcnews .com/storyline/lethal-injection/careless-cavalier-grand-jury-issues -scathing-report-botched-oklahoma-executions-n577281; In the Matter of the Multicounty Grand Jury, State of Oklahoma, District Court of Oklahoma County, Interim Report Number 14, May 19, 2016, at www .ok.gov/oag/documents/MCGJ%20-%20Interim%20Report%205-19 -16.pdf.

255. More Than the Richard Glossip Case: For the Constitution, for Social Justice, for Reasons Pragmatic and Humane, Put the Death Penalty into Mothballs," The City Sentinel (Oklahoma City, OK), Feb. 14, 2016, at http://city-sentinel.com/2016/02/more-than-the-richard-glossip -case-for-the-constitution-for-social-justice-for-reasons-pragmatic -and-humane-put-the-death-penalty-into-mothballs.

256. *Marbury v. Madison,* 5 U.S. (1 Cranch) 137, 177–78 (1803).

257. Text of the Oaths of Office for Supreme Court Justices, Supreme Court of the United States, at www.supremecourt.gov/about /oath/textoftheoathsofoffice2009.aspx.

258. William J. Brennan Jr., *Constitutional Adjudication and the Death Penalty: A View from the Court,* 100 Harv. L. Rev. 313, 331 (1986).

259. John D. Bessler, *Tinkering Around the Edges: The Supreme Court's Death Penalty Jurisprudence,* 49 Am. Crim. L. Rev. 1913 (2012).

260. Paul Zummo, Thomas Jefferson's America: Democracy, Progress, and the Quest for Perfection, Ph.D. thesis, Catholic University of America, Washington, D.C. (2008), pp. 115–16.

261. Erik Eckholm, Pfizer Blocks the Use of Its Drugs in Executions, N.Y. Times, May 13, 2016; Associated Press, Pfizer Says It Won't Allow Its Drugs to Be Used in Executions: Here's What that

Means, L.A. Times, May 14, 2016; Maura Dolan, The Drugs to Execute Criminals Could Cost Hundreds of Thousands of Dollars, California Prison Agency Records Show, L.A. Times, May 10, 2016; Chuck Lindell, Court Debates Impact of Keeping Execution Drug Suppliers Secret, Austin-American Statesman, May 11, 2016; Joe Duggan, Ricketts Stops Trying to Import Death Penalty Drugs for Now, Omaha.com, Dec. 7, 2015, at www.omaha.com/news/nebraska/ricketts-stops-trying -to-import-death-penalty-drugs-for-now/article_85e2a404-9ae5-11e5 -8d92-7774506a50cb.html; Astrid Galvan & Justin Pritchard, Feds Confiscate Lethal-Injection Drugs Imported by 2 States, Seattle Times, Oct. 23, 2015; Eric Berger, *Lethal Injection Secrecy and Eighth Amendment Due Process*, 55 B.C. L. REV. 1367, 1388 (2014); Clay Calvert, Emma Morehart, Kéran Billaud & Kevin Bruckenstein, *Access to Information About Lethal Injections: A First Amendment Theory Perspective on Creating a New Constitutional Right*, 38 HASTINGS COMM. & ENT. L.J. 1, 22 (2016).

JUSTICE BREYER'S DISSENT
IN *GLOSSIP V. GROSS*

1. Amdt. 8.
2. *Atkins v. Virginia*, 536 U.S. 304, 311 (2002). [*Ed. note:* George Jeffreys (1648–1689), an English lawyer knighted in 1677, became Lord Chief Justice of the King's Bench in 1683. After King James II took the throne in 1685, he named Jeffreys as Lord Chancellor. Jeffreys is most remembered for presiding over Algernon Sidney's treason trial (1683) and the "Bloody Assizes" (1685), a series of judicial sittings in southwest England to try nearly 2,000 prisoners taken captive in the failed Monmouth Rebellion. The Duke of Monmouth was executed on July 15, 1685, and the first assizes began on August 25, 1685. To expedite the trials, rebels pleading guilty were offered the prospect of the king's mercy, while those pleading not guilty were told they would be summarily executed if convicted. The first mass convictions and executions took place on September 5, 1685, in Dorchester, and some who pled guilty were executed despite their pleas. Known for his corrupt and cruel actions, Jeffreys ordered the hanging—and drawing and

quartering and gibbeting—of scores of rebels. One elderly woman, Lady Alice Lisle, was ordered to be burned alive for sheltering a rebel fugitive, although a plea to the king led to a commutation of that sentence to beheading. Following the Glorious Revolution of 1688, which overthrew James II, the English Bill of Rights was adopted by the Westminster Parliament on December 16, 1689. Jeffreys, while imprisoned in the Tower of London, died on April 18, 1689. Christopher L. Scott, *The Maligned Militia: The West Country Militia of the Monmouth Rebellion, 1685* (Surrey, England: Ashgate, 2015), p. 305; Ronald H. Fritze & William B. Robison, eds., *Historical Dictionary of Stuart England, 1603–1689* (Westport, CT: Greenwood, Press, 1996), p. 48; Thomas Seccombe, ed., *Lives of Twelve Bad Men: Original Studies of Eminent Scoundrels by Various Hands* (London: T. Fisher Unwin, 1894), pp. 73, 77–86; Henry Fielding, *Contributions to The Champion and Related Writings* (Oxford: Clarendon Press, W. B. Coley, ed. 2003), p. 547 n.1; Ralph Paul Bieber, *The Lords of Trade and Plantations 1675–1696* (Allentown, PA: H. Ray Haas & Co., 1919), p. 35; Steve Pincus, *1688: The First Modern Revolution* (New Haven: Yale University Press, 2009), pp. 42, 481; Bruno Aguilera-Barchet, *A History of Western Public Law: Between Nation and State* (Cham, Switzerland: Springer, 2015), p. 299 & n.37; John Lord Campbell, *Lives of the Lord Chancellors and Keepers of the Great Seal of England, from the Earliest Times Till the Reign of King George IV* (London: John Murray, 5th ed., 1868), Vol. IV, p. 414.]

3. *See* 4 W. Blackstone, *Commentaries on the Laws of England* 369–70 (1769) (listing mutilation and dismembering, among other punishments). [*Ed. note:* William Blackstone (1723–1780), an English jurist and penal reformer, became the first Vinerian Professor of English Law at Oxford in 1758. His *Commentaries on the Laws of England*, published between 1765 and 1769, were widely read—and extremely influential—in the United States. Among other things, Blackstone played a pivotal role in the promotion of penitentiaries. Wilfrid R. Prest, *William Blackstone: Law and Letters in the Eighteenth Century* (Oxford: Oxford University Press, 2008), pp. 1–5, 13, 139, 279, 297–301; Mark Weston Janis, *America and the Law of Nations 1776–1939* (Oxford: Oxford University Press, 2010), pp. 2, 43.]

4. *See Gregg v. Georgia,* 428 U.S. 153, 187 (1976) (joint opinion of Stewart, Powell, and Stevens, JJ.); *Proffitt v. Florida,* 428 U.S. 242, 247 (1976) (joint opinion of Stewart, Powell, and Stevens, JJ.); *Jurek v. Texas,* 428 U.S. 262, 268 (1976) (joint opinion of Stewart, Powell, and Stevens, JJ.); *but cf. Woodson v. North Carolina,* 428 U.S. 280, 303 (1976) (plurality opinion) (striking down mandatory death penalty); *Roberts v. Louisiana,* 428 U.S. 325, 331 (1976) (plurality opinion) (similar).

5. U.S. Const., Amdt. 8. [*Ed. note*: This is, certainly, not the first time that Justices Breyer and Ginsburg have indicated their aversion to death sentences. For years, they have voted to restrict the death penalty's use or to make it more difficult for a death sentence to be meted out. Ginsburg wrote the opinion, with Breyer concurring in the judgment, holding that a capital defendant has a right to have *a jury*, rather than a single *judge*, decide on the existence of an aggravating factor making a defendant eligible for the death penalty. *Ring v. Arizona,* 536 U.S. 584, 588, 595 (2002); *id.* at 614 (Breyer, J., concurring in the judgment). Justices Breyer and Ginsburg voted with Justice John Paul Stevens to make the intellectually disabled ineligible for the death penalty. *Atkins v. Virginia,* 536 U.S. 304, 305–306 (2002); *see also Hall v. Florida,* 134 S. Ct. 1986, 1990 (2014). They joined Justice Sandra Day O'Connor's majority opinion holding that the failure to consider a defendant's impaired intellectual functioning in a capital trial violated the Eighth Amendment. *Tennard v. Dretke,* 542 U.S. 274, 275–76 (2004). They joined Justice Anthony Kennedy in forbidding the death penalty's use on juvenile offenders. *Roper v. Simmons,* 543 U.S. 551, 554–60 (2005) (joined by Justices Breyer and Ginsburg); *see also id.* at 587 (Stevens, J., concurring; joined by Justice Ginsburg). They joined Justice Kennedy again in allowing the consideration of new evidence of innocence in a capital case. *House v. Bell,* 547 U.S. 518 (2006); *see also* Linda E. Carter, Ellen S. Kreitzberg, & Scott Howe, *Understanding Capital Punishment* (New Providence, NJ: LexisNexis, 3d ed. 2012), § 17.02[B][2] n.64 (noting that the death row inmate, Paul House, later released from prison, presented evidence of his innocence, including a DNA test showing that semen found on the murder victim's clothes belonged to the victim's husband, not to House). And they joined Justice

Kennedy yet again in declaring the death penalty unconstitutional for the crime of nonhomicidal child rape. In that case, Justice Kennedy wrote, "When the law punishes by death, it risks its own sudden descent into brutality, transgressing the constitutional commitment to decency and restraint." *Kennedy v. Louisiana,* 554 U.S. 407, 411, 420 (2008).]

6. *Woodson,* 428 U.S., at 305 (plurality opinion).

7. *Ibid.*

8. *Cf. Kansas v. Marsh,* 548 U.S. 163, 207–11 (2006) (Souter, J., dissenting) (DNA exonerations constitute "a new body of fact" when considering the constitutionality of capital punishment).

9. *See, e.g.,* Liebman, Fatal Injustice; Carlos DeLuna's Execution Shows That a Faster, Cheaper Death Penalty Is a Dangerous Idea, L.A. Times, June 1, 2012, p. A19 (describing results of a 4-year investigation, later published as *The Wrong Carlos: Anatomy of a Wrongful Execution* (2014), that led its authors to conclude that Carlos DeLuna, sentenced to death and executed in 1989, six years after his arrest in Texas for stabbing a single mother to death in a convenience store, was innocent); Grann, Trial By Fire: Did Texas Execute an Innocent Man? The New Yorker, Sept. 7, 2009, p. 42 (describing evidence that Cameron Todd Willingham was convicted, and ultimately executed in 2004, for the apparently motiveless murder of his three children as the result of invalid scientific analysis of the scene of the house fire that killed his children). *See also, e.g.,* Press Release: Gov. Ritter Grants Posthumous Pardon in Case Dating Back to 1930s, Jan. 7, 2011, p. 1 (Colorado Governor granted full and unconditional posthumous pardon to Joe Arridy, a man with an IQ of 46 who was executed in 1936, because, according to the Governor, "an overwhelming body of evidence indicates the 23-year-old Arridy was innocent, including false and coerced confessions, the likelihood that Arridy was not in Pueblo at the time of the killing, and an admission of guilt by someone else"); R. Warden, *Wilkie Collins's The Dead Alive: The Novel, the Case, and Wrongful Convictions* 157–58 (2005) (in 1987, Nebraska Governor Bob Kerrey pardoned William Jackson Marion, who had been executed a century earlier for the murder of John Cameron, a man who later turned up alive; the alleged victim, Cameron, had gone

to Mexico to avoid a shotgun wedding). [*Ed. note:* Rob Warden, the author of the book cited by Justice Breyer and published by Northwestern University Press in Evanston, Illinois, is an award-winning journalist and now the Executive Director, Emeritus, of Northwestern's Center on Wrongful Convictions. He exposed many wrongful convictions in Illinois.]

10. *Atkins,* 536 U.S., at 320, n.25; National Registry of Exonerations, at www.law.umich.edu/special/exoneration/Pages/about.aspx (all Internet materials as visited June 25, 2015, and available in Clerk of Court's case file).

11. *Ibid.*; National Registry of Exonerations, Exonerations in the United States, 1989–2012, pp. 6–7 (2012) (Exonerations 2012 Report) (defining exoneration); *accord*, Death Penalty Information Center (DPIC), Innocence: List of Those Freed from Death Row, at www.deathpenaltyinfo.org/innocence-and-death-penalty (DPIC Innocence List) (calculating, under a slightly different definition of exoneration, the number of exonerations since 1973 as 154).

12. National Registry of Exonerations, Exonerations in 2014, p. 2 (2015).

13. Katz & Eckholm, DNA Evidence Clears Two Men in 1983 Murder, N.Y. Times, Sept. 3, 2014, p. A1. [*Ed. note:* On June 30, 1994, the U.S. Supreme Court declined to consider the case of Henry Lee "Buddy" McCollum, convicted and sentenced to death for the rape and murder of an 11-year-old girl. *See State v. McCollum,* 433 S.E.2d 144 (N.C. 1993); *McCollum v. North Carolina,* 512 U.S. 1254 (1994). Only Justice Harry Blackmun dissented from the Supreme Court's refusal to hear the case. In that dissent, Blackmun acknowledged that McCollum was "sentenced to be executed for his part in a brutal crime"—"the rape and murder of an 11-year-old girl." *Id.* at 1254–55 (Blackmun, J., dissenting). But Blackmun had announced earlier that year, in his dissent in *Callins v. Collins,* 510 U.S. 1141, 1143–59 (1994) (Blackmun, J., dissenting from denial of cert.), that he would no longer "tinker with the machinery of death." Blackmun, who had come to believe that the death penalty is unconstitutional, also pointed out that McCollum had an IQ of "between 60 and 69 and the mental age of a 9-year-old." "That our system of capital punishment would single out Buddy

McCollum to die for this brutal crime," Blackmun wrote, "only confirms my conclusion that the death penalty experiment has failed." *McCollum*, 512 U.S. at 1255 (Blackmun, J., dissenting). In a concurring opinion in *Callins v. Collins*, Justice Antonin Scalia had specifically pointed to the case of Henry Lee McCollum as a reason for retaining the death penalty. In that concurrence, Justice Scalia noted "[h]ow enviable a quiet death by lethal injection" was compared to "the case of the 11-year-old girl raped by four men and then killed by stuffing her panties down her throat." *Callins*, 510 U.S. at 1143 (Scalia, J., concurring). In 2014, 30 years after his murder and rape conviction, DNA evidence exonerated McCollum, leading to his release, along with the release of his mentally disabled half-brother. Jonathan M. Katz & Erik Eckholm, "DNA Evidence Clears Two Men in 1983 Murder," N.Y. Times, Sept. 2, 2014.]

14. *Hinton v. Alabama,* 134 S. Ct. 1081 (2014) (*per curiam*); Blinder, Alabama Man on Death Row for Three Decades Is Freed as State's Case Erodes, N.Y. Times, Apr. 4, 2014, p. A11.

15. Stroud, Lead Prosecutor Apologizes for Role in Sending Man to Death Row, Shreveport Times, Mar. 27, 2015. [*Ed. note:* Sadly, Glenn Ford—who spent nearly 30 years on death row for a murder he didn't commit—died of lung cancer the year following his release from Louisiana's death row. "Exonerated Convict Glenn Ford Succumbs to Lung Cancer at 65," The Times-Picayune, June 29, 2015.]

16. Exonerations 2012 Report 15–16, and nn.24–26.

17. *See* Gross, Jacoby, Matheson, Montgomery, & Patil, *Exonerations in the United States 1989 Through 2003,* 95 J. Crim. L. & C. 523, 531–33 (2005); Gross & O'Brien, *Frequency and Predictors of False Conviction: Why We Know So Little, and New Data on Capital Cases,* 5 J. Empirical L. Studies 927, 956–57 (2008) (noting that, in comparing those who were exonerated from death row to other capital defendants who were not so exonerated, the initial police investigations tended to be shorter for those exonerated); *see also* B. Garrett, *Convicting the Innocent: Where Criminal Prosecutions Go Wrong* (2011) (discussing other common causes of wrongful convictions generally including false confessions, mistaken eyewitness testimony, untruthful jailhouse informants, and ineffective defense counsel).

18. Possley, Prosecutor Accused of Misconduct in Death Penalty Case, Washington Post, Mar. 19, 2015, p. A3.

19. Stroud, *supra*.

20. *See* Rozelle, *The Principled Executioner: Capital Juries' Bias and the Benefits of True Bifurcation,* 38 Ariz. S. L.J. 769, 772–93, 807 (2006) (summarizing research and concluding that "[f]or over fifty years, empirical investigation has demonstrated that death qualification skews juries toward guilt and death"); Note, *Mandatory Voir Dire Questions in Capital Cases: A Potential Solution to the Biases of Death Qualification,* 10 Roger Williams Univ. L. Rev. 211, 214–23 (2004) (similar). [*Ed. note:* The U.S. Supreme Court has held that courts must look to the "evolving standards of decency that mark the progress of a maturing society" to determine whether the Eighth Amendment permits a particular punishment. *Trop v. Dulles,* 356 U.S. 86, 101 (1958); *Roper v. Simmons,* 543 U.S. 551, 560–61 (2005); *Hall v. Florida,* 134 S. Ct. 1986, 1992 (2014). In gauging those "evolving standards," the Supreme Court treats jury verdicts as "a significant and reliable objective index of contemporary values" because juries are "so directly involved." *Gregg v. Georgia,* 428 U.S. 153, 181 (1976); *Coker v. Georgia,* 433 U.S. 584, 595 (1977). Yet, the Supreme Court has held that "death qualification," which studies have long shown disproportionately excludes minorities, women, Democrats, Catholics, Jews, Unitarians, and young people, is constitutional, and that excluding death penalty opponents from sitting in judgment in capital cases is acceptable even if it "produces juries somewhat more 'conviction-prone' than 'non-death-qualified' juries." *Lockhart v. McCree,* 476 U.S. 162, 177 (1986); *Wainwright v. Witt,* 469 U.S. 412, 424 (1985); Welsh S. White, *The Constitutional Invalidity of Convictions Imposed by Death-Qualified Juries,* 58 Cornell L. Rev. 1176, 1185 (1973); Justin D. Levinson, Robert J. Smith, & Danielle M. Young, *Devaluing Death: An Empirical Study of Implicit Racial Bias on Jury-Eligible Citizens in Six Death Penalty States,* 89 N.Y.U. L. Rev. 513, 558–60 (2014); Meghan J. Ryan, *The Missing Jury: The Neglected Role of Juries in Eighth Amendment Punishments Clause Determinations,* 64 Fla. L. Rev. 549, 582 n.195 (2012); Richard C. Dieter, *A Crisis of Confidence: Americans' Doubts about the Death Penalty* (June 2007), p. 2.]

21. *See* Garrett, *supra,* at 7.

22. FBI, National Press Releases, FBI Testimony on Microscopic Hair Analysis Contained Errors in at Least 90 Percent of Cases in Ongoing Review, Apr. 20, 2015. *See also* Hsu, FBI Admits Errors at Trials: False Matches on Crime-Scene Hair, Washington Post, Apr. 19, 2015, p. A1 (in the District of Columbia, which does not have the death penalty, five of seven defendants in cases with flawed hair analysis testimony were eventually exonerated).

23. *See* Gross, O'Brien, Hu, & Kennedy, *Rate of False Conviction of Criminal Defendants Who Are Sentenced to Death,* 111 Proceeding of the National Academy of Sciences 7230 (2014) (full-scale study of all death sentences from 1973 through 2004 estimating that 4.1% of those sentenced to death are actually innocent); Risinger, *Innocents Convicted: An Empirically Justified Factual Wrongful Conviction Rate,* 97 J. Crim. L. & C. 761 (2007) (examination of DNA exonerations in death penalty cases for murder-rapes between 1982 and 1989 suggesting an analogous rate of between 3.3% and 5%).

24. Gelman, Liebman, West, & Kiss, *A Broken System: The Persistent Patterns of Reversals of Death Sentences in the United States,* 1 J. Empirical L. Studies 209, 217 (2004).

25. *Id.,* at 232.

26. *Ibid.*

27. *See* Earley, *A Pink Cadillac, An IQ of 63, and A Fourteen-Year-Old from South Carolina: Why I Can No Longer Support the Death Penalty,* 49 U. Rich. L. Rev. 811, 813 (2015) ("I have come to the conclusion that the death penalty is based on a false utopian premise. That false premise is that we have had, do have, will have 100% accuracy in death penalty convictions and executions"); Earley, I Oversaw 36 Executions. Even Death Penalty Supporters Can Push for Change, Guardian, May 12, 2014 (Earley presided over 36 executions as Virginia Attorney General from 1998–2001); *but see ante,* at 2747–48 (SCALIA, J., concurring) (apparently finding no special constitutional problem arising from the fact that the execution of an innocent person is irreversible). [*Ed. note*: In his concurring opinion, Justice Scalia emphasized that "it is *convictions*, not *punishments*, that are unreliable." *Glossip v. Gross,* 135 S. Ct. 2726, 2747–48 (Scalia, J., concurring) (italics in original).]

28. 408 U.S. 238 (1972) (*per curiam*).

29. *Furman*, 408 U.S., at 309–10 (concurring opinion). *See also id.*, at 310 ("[T]he Eighth and Fourteenth Amendments cannot tolerate the infliction of a sentence of death under legal systems that permit this unique penalty to be so wantonly and so freakishly imposed"); *id.*, at 313 (White, J., concurring) ("[T]he death penalty is exacted with great infrequency even for the most atrocious crimes and . . . there is no meaningful basis for distinguishing the few cases in which it is imposed from the many cases in which it is not").

30. *Gregg*, 428 U.S., at 188 (joint opinion of Stewart, Powell, and Stevens, JJ.); *see also id.*, at 189 ("[W]here discretion is afforded a sentencing body on a matter so grave as the determination of whether a human life should be taken or spared, that discretion must be suitably directed and limited so as to minimize the risk of wholly arbitrary and capricious action"); *Godfrey v. Georgia,* 446 U.S. 420, 428 (1980) (plurality opinion) (similar).

31. *Kansas v. Marsh*, 548 U.S., at 206 (dissenting opinion); *see also Roper v. Simmons,* 543 U.S. 551, 568 (2005) ("Capital punishment must be limited to those offenders who commit a narrow category of the most serious crimes and whose extreme culpability makes them the most deserving of execution" (internal quotation marks omitted)); *Kennedy v. Louisiana,* 554 U.S. 407, 420 (2008) (citing *Roper, supra*, at 568).

32. *Eddings v. Oklahoma,* 455 U.S. 104, 112 (1982).

33. Donohue, *An Empirical Evaluation of the Connecticut Death Penalty System Since 1973: Are There Unlawful Racial, Gender, and Geographic Disparities?* 11 J. Empirical Legal Studies 637 (2014).

34. *Id.*, at 641–43.

35. *Id.*, at 641.

36. *Id.*, at 643–45.

37. *Id.*, at 678–79.

38. *See* GAO, *Report to the Senate and House Committees on the Judiciary: Death Penalty Sentencing* 5 (GAO/GGD–90–57, 1990) (82% of the 28 studies conducted between 1972 and 1990 found that race of victim influences capital murder charge or death sentence, a "finding . . . remarkably consistent across data sets, states, data collection methods, and analytic techniques"); Shatz & Dalton, *Challenging the Death Penalty with Statistics:* Furman, McCleskey, *and a Single*

County Case Study, 34 Cardozo L. Rev. 1227, 1245–51 (2013) (same conclusion drawn from 20 plus studies conducted between 1990 and 2013).

39. *Id.,* at 1251–53 (citing many studies).

40. *See id.,* at 1253–56.

41. Smith, *The Geography of the Death Penalty and its Ramifications,* 92 B. U. L. Rev. 227, 231–32 (2012) (hereinafter Smith); *see also* Donohue, *supra,* at 673 ("[T]he single most important influence from 1973–2007 explaining whether a death-eligible defendant [in Connecticut] would be sentenced to death was whether the crime occurred in Waterbury [County]").

42. Smith 233.

43. DPIC, *The 2% Death Penalty: How a Minority of Counties Produce Most Death Cases at Enormous Costs to All* 9 (Oct. 2013).

44. *See, e.g.,* Goelzhauser, *Prosecutorial Discretion Under Resource Constraints: Budget Allocations and Local Death–Charging Decisions,* 96 Judicature 161, 162–63 (2013); Barnes, Sloss, & Thaman, *Place Matters (Most): An Empirical Study of Prosecutorial Decision-Making in Death-Eligible Cases,* 51 Ariz. L. Rev. 305 (2009) (analyzing Missouri); Donohue, *An Empirical Evaluation of the Connecticut Death Penalty System,* at 681 (Connecticut); Marceau, Kamin, & Foglia, *Death Eligibility in Colorado: Many Are Called, Few Are Chosen,* 84 U. Colo. L. Rev. 1069 (2013) (Colorado); Shatz & Dalton, *supra,* at 1260–61 (Alameda County).

45. *See, e.g.,* Smith 258–65 (counties with higher death-sentencing rates tend to have weaker public defense programs); Liebman & Clarke, *Minority Practice, Majority's Burden: The Death Penalty Today,* 9 Ohio S. J. Crim. L. 255, 274 (2011) (hereinafter Liebman & Clarke) (similar); *see generally* Bright, *Counsel for the Poor: The Death Sentence Not for the Worst Crime But for the Worst Lawyer,* 103 Yale L. J. 1835 (1994).

46. *See, e.g.,* Levinson, Smith, & Young, *Devaluing Death: An Empirical Study of Implicit Racial Bias on Jury-Eligible Citizens in Six Death Penalty States,* 89 N.Y.U. L. Rev. 513, 533–36 (2014) (summarizing research on this point); *see also* Shatz & Dalton, *supra,* at 1275 (describing research finding that death-sentencing rates were

lowest in counties with the highest nonwhite population); *cf.* Cohen
& Smith, *The Racial Geography of the Federal Death Penalty,* 85
Wash. L. Rev. 425 (2010) (arguing that the federal death penalty is
sought disproportionately where the federal district, from which the
jury will be drawn, has a dramatic racial difference from the county in
which the federal crime occurred).

47. *See Woodward v. Alabama,* 134 S. Ct. 405, 408 (2013) (SOTO-
MAYOR, J., dissenting from denial of certiorari) (noting that empirical
evidence suggests that, when Alabama judges reverse jury recommendations, these "judges, who are elected in partisan proceedings, appear to have succumbed to electoral pressures"); *Harris v. Alabama,*
513 U.S. 504, 519 (1995) (Stevens, J., dissenting) (similar); Gelman,
1 J. Empirical L. Studies, at 247 (elected state judges are less likely to
reverse flawed verdicts in capital cases in small towns than in larger
communities).

48. *Ante,* at 2752–55 (concurring opinion). [*Ed. note:* In his concurring opinion in *Glossip,* Justice Thomas pointed to cases involving
horrific murders and rapes. In that concurrence, Thomas—joined by
Justice Scalia—argued that the Court had "misinterpreted the Eighth
Amendment" in granting relief based on "unfounded" Eighth Amendment claims. In particular, Thomas and Scalia asserted that the Supreme
Court should not have granted Eighth Amendment relief to juvenile
offenders, the intellectually disabled, or nonhomicidal rapists. *Glossip,*
135 S. Ct. at 2752–55 (Thomas, J., concurring).]

49. 428 U.S., at 304–305.

50. *Supra,* at 2759–60. [*Ed. note:* This citation, citing pages in the
Supreme Court Reporter, references an earlier portion of Justice Breyer's
own dissent in *Glossip. See Glossip,* 135 S. Ct. at 2759–60 (Breyer, J.,
dissent).]

51. *See Gregg,* 428 U.S., at 195 (joint opinion of Stewart, Powell,
and Stevens, JJ.) ("[T]he concerns expressed in *Furman* that the penalty
of death not be imposed in an arbitrary or capricious manner can be
met").

52. *Id.,* at 199, and n.50 (joint opinion of Stewart, Powell, and
Stevens, JJ.); *McCleskey v. Kemp,* 481 U.S. 279, 307–308, and n.28,
311–12 (1987).

53. Smith, *The Supreme Court and the Politics of Death,* 94 Va. L. Rev. 283, 355 (2008) ("Capital defenders are notoriously underfunded, particularly in states . . . that lead the nation in executions"); American Bar Assn. (ABA) *Guidelines for the Appointment and Performance of Defense Counsel in Death Penalty Cases,* Guideline 9.1, Commentary (rev. ed. Feb. 2003), in 31 Hofstra L. Rev. 913, 985 (2003) ("[C]ompensation of attorneys for death penalty representation remains notoriously inadequate").

54. *See, e.g., Harris, supra.*

55. *See Callins v. Collins,* 510 U.S. 1141, 1153 (1994) (Blackmun, J., dissenting from denial of certiorari) ("Perhaps it should not be surprising that the biases and prejudices that infect society generally would influence the determination of who is sentenced to death").

56. *See, e.g., Penry v. Lynaugh,* 492 U.S. 302, 319 (1989); *Lockett v. Ohio,* 438 U.S. 586, 604–605 (1978) (opinion of Burger, C.J.); *Woodson,* 428 U.S., at 304–305 (plurality opinion).

57. *Pulley v. Harris,* 465 U.S. 37 (1984).

58. *See* Kaufman-Osborn, *Capital Punishment, Proportionality Review, and Claims of Fairness (with Lessons from Washington State),* 79 Wash. L. Rev. 775, 791–92 (2004) (after *Pulley,* many States repealed their statutes requiring comparative proportionality review, and most state high courts "reduced proportionality review to a perfunctory exercise" (internal quotation marks omitted)).

59. *Cf. Godfrey,* 446 U.S., at 433 (plurality opinion) ("There is no principled way to distinguish this case, in which the death penalty was imposed, from the many cases in which it was not").

60. *Compare State v. Badgett,* 361 N.C. 234 (2007), and Pet. for Cert. in *Badgett v. North Carolina,* O.T. 2006, No. 07-6156, *with* Charbonneau, Andre Edwards Sentenced to Life in Prison for 2001 Murder, WRAL, Mar. 26, 2004, at www.wral.com/news/local/story /109648. [*Ed. note:* The original version of the sentence in Justice Breyer's dissenting opinion that corresponds with this note ends with a period instead of a question mark. A question mark has been substituted for the period.]

61. *Compare Commonwealth v. Boxley,* 596 Pa. 620 (2008), and Pet. for Cert., O.T. 2008, No. 08-6172, *with* Shea, Judge Gives Con-

secutive Life Sentences for Triple Murder, Philadelphia Inquirer, June 29, 2004, p. B5.

62. *See* Donohue, *Capital Punishment in Connecticut, 1973–2007: A Comprehensive Evaluation from 4686 Murders to One Execution,* pp. 128–34 (2013), at http://works.bepress.com/john_donohue/87.

63. *Roper,* 543 U.S., at 568.

64. *Hall v. Florida,* 134 S. Ct. 1986, 2001 (2014).

65. *Gregg,* 428 U.S., at 187 (joint opinion of Stewart, Powell, and Stevens, JJ.); *Furman,* 408 U.S., at 306 (Stewart, J., concurring) (death "differs from all other forms of criminal punishment, not in degree but in kind"); *Woodson, supra,* at 305 (plurality opinion) ("Death, in its finality, differs more from life imprisonment than a 100-year prison term differs from one of only a year or two").

66. DPIC, Execution List 2014, at www.deathpenaltyinfo.org/execution-list-2014 (showing an average delay of 17 years, 7 months).

67. Tr. of Oral Arg. in *Hall v. Florida,* O.T. 2013, No. 12-10882, p. 46.

68. *See* Aarons, *Can Inordinate Delay Between a Death Sentence and Execution Constitute Cruel and Unusual Punishment?* 29 Seton Hall L. Rev. 147, 181 (1998).

69. *See* Dept. of Justice, Bureau of Justice Statistics (BJS), T. Snell, *Capital Punishment, 2013—Statistical Tables* 14 (Table 10) (rev. Dec. 2014) (hereinafter BJS 2013 Stats).

70. DPIC, Execution List 2014, *supra.*

71. BJS 2013 Stats, at 14, 18 (Tables 11 and 15).

72. *See Johnson v. Bredesen,* 558 U.S. 1067, 1069 (2009) (Stevens, J., statement respecting denial of certiorari). [*Ed. note*: For many years, Justice Breyer has called upon his Supreme Court colleagues to consider whether extended stays on death row violate the Eighth Amendment's Cruel and Unusual Punishments Clause. In dissenting from a denial of certiorari in 1998 for an inmate who had spent more than two decades on death row, Breyer wrote, "Twenty-three years under sentence of death is unusual—whether one takes as a measuring rod current practice or the practice in this country and in England at the time our Constitution was written." "As Justice Stevens has

previously pointed out," Breyer observed, citing his colleague's prior opinion in *Lackey v. Texas*, "executions carried out after delays of this magnitude may prove particularly cruel." *Elledge v. Florida*, 525 U.S. 944 (1998) (Breyer, J., dissenting from denial of cert.) (citing *Lackey v. Texas*, 514 U.S. 1045 (1995) (opinion respecting denial of cert.)). On multiple occasions since *Elledge*, Breyer has renewed his call for the nation's highest court to take up whether prolonged stays on death row violate the Eighth Amendment. *Muhammad v. Florida*, 134 S. Ct. 894 (2014) (Breyer, J., dissenting statement); *Valle v. Florida*, 132 S. Ct. 1 (2011) (Breyer, J., dissenting from denial of stay); *Johnson v. Bredesen*, 558 U.S. 1067 (2009) (statement of Justice Stevens, with whom Justice Breyer joins, respecting denial of certiorari); *Knight v. Florida*, 528 U.S. 990, 993 (1999) (Breyer, J., dissenting from denial of certiorari).]

73. *Ibid.*; *Gomez v. Fierro*, 519 U.S. 918 (1996) (Stevens, J., dissenting) (excessive delays from sentencing to execution can themselves "constitute cruel and unusual punishment prohibited by the Eighth Amendment"); *see also Lackey v. Texas*, 514 U.S. 1045 (1995) (memorandum of Stevens, J., respecting denial of certiorari); *Knight v. Florida*, 528 U.S. 990, 993 (1999) (BREYER, J., dissenting from denial of certiorari).

74. *Johnson, supra*, at 1069; *Thompson v. McNeil*, 556 U.S. 1114, 1115 (2009) (statement of Stevens, J., respecting denial of certiorari). [*Ed. note:* The asserted rationales for the death penalty are discussed later in Justice Breyer's *Glossip* dissent. In a prior case, Justice John Paul Stevens—now retired—wrote that "delaying an execution does not further public purposes of retribution and deterrence but only diminishes whatever possible benefit society might receive from petitioner's death." "It would therefore be appropriate," he observed, "to conclude that a punishment of death after significant delay is 'so totally without penological justification that it results in the gratuitous infliction of suffering.'" *Thompson v. McNeil*, 556 U.S. 1114 (2009) (Stevens, J., statement respecting denial of cert.) (quoting *Gregg v. Georgia*, 428 U.S. 153, 183 (1976) (joint opinion of Justices Stewart, Powell, and Stevens).]

75. American Civil Liberties Union (ACLU), *A Death Before Dying: Solitary Confinement on Death Row* 5 (July 2013) (ACLU Report).

76. *See id.*, at 2, 4; *ABA Standards for Criminal Justice: Treatment of Prisoners* 6 (3d ed. 2011).

77. *See, e.g.,* Haney, *Mental Health Issues in Long-Term Solitary and "Supermax" Confinement,* 49 Crime & Delinquency 124, 130 (2003) (cataloguing studies finding that solitary confinement can cause prisoners to experience "anxiety, panic, rage, loss of control, paranoia, hallucinations, and self-mutilations," among many other symptoms); Grassian, *Psychiatric Effects of Solitary Confinement,* 22 Wash U. J. L. & Policy 325, 331 (2006) ("[E]ven a few days of solitary confinement will predictably shift the [brain's] electroencephalogram (EEG) pattern toward an abnormal pattern characteristic of stupor and delirium"); *accord, In re Medley,* 134 U.S. 160, 167–68 (1890); *see also Davis v. Ayala,* 135 S. Ct. 2187 (2015) (KENNEDY, J., concurring).

78. *Medley, supra,* at 172.

79. *Supra,* at 2764–65. [*Ed. note:* This citation, citing pages in the *Supreme Court Reporter,* references an earlier portion of Justice Breyer's own dissent in *Glossip. See Glossip,* 135 S. Ct. at 2764–65 (Breyer, J., dissenting).]

80. *See, e.g.,* Pet. for Cert. in *Suárez Medina v. Texas,* O.T. 2001, No. 02-5752, pp. 35–36 (filed Aug. 13, 2002) ("On fourteen separate occasions since Mr. Suárez Medina's death sentence was imposed, he has been informed of the time, date, and manner of his death. At least eleven times, he has been asked to describe the disposal of his bodily remains"); Lithwick, Cruel but not Unusual, Slate, Apr. 1, 2011, at www.slate.com/articles/news_and_politics/jurisprudence/2011/04 /cruel_ but_not_unusual.html (John Thompson had seven death warrants signed before he was exonerated); *see also, e.g.,* WFMZ-TV 69 News, Michael John Parrish's Execution Warrant Signed by Governor Corbett (Aug. 18, 2014), at www.wfmz.com/news/Regional-Poconos -Coal/Local/michael-john-parrishs-execution-warrant-signed-by -governor-corbett/27595356 (former Pennsylvania Governor signed 36 death warrants in his first 3.5 years in office even though Pennsylvania has not carried out an execution since 1999).

81. *See* Robertson, With Hours to Go, Execution Is Postponed, N.Y. Times, Apr. 8, 2015, p. A17.

82. Nave, Why Does the State Still Want to Kill Willie Jerome Manning? Jackson Free Press, Apr. 29, 2015.

83. *See, e.g.,* Martin, Randall Adams, 61, Dies; Freed With Help of Film, N.Y. Times, June 26, 2011, p. 24 (Randall Adams: stayed by this

Court three days before execution; later exonerated); N. Davies, *White Lies* 231, 292, 298, 399 (1991) (Clarence Lee Brandley: execution stayed twice, once 6 days and once 10 days before; later exonerated); M. Edds, *An Expendable Man* 93 (2003) (Earl Washington, Jr.: stayed 9 days before execution; later exonerated).

84. *See, e.g.,* ACLU Report 8; Rountree, *Volunteers for Execution: Directions for Further Research into Grief, Culpability, and Legal Structures,* 82 UMKC L. Rev. 295 (2014) (11% of those executed have dropped appeals and volunteered); ACLU Report 3 (account of " 'guys who dropped their appeals because of the intolerable conditions' ").

85. Strafer, *Volunteering for Execution: Competency, Voluntariness and the Propriety of Third Party Intervention,* 74 J. Crim. L. & C. 860, 869 (1983).

86. *Id.,* at 872, n.44 (35% of those confined on death row in Florida attempted suicide).

87. *See, e.g., Johnson,* 558 U.S., at 1069 (statement of Stevens, J.) (delay "subjects death row inmates to decades of especially severe, dehumanizing conditions of confinement"); *Furman,* 408 U.S., at 288 (Brennan, J., concurring) ("long wait between the imposition of sentence and the actual infliction of death" is "inevitable" and often "exacts a frightful toll"); *Solesbee v. Balkcom,* 339 U.S. 9, 14 (1950) (Frankfurter, J., dissenting) ("In the history of murder, the onset of insanity while awaiting execution of a death sentence is not a rare phenomenon"); *People v. Anderson,* 6 Cal.3d 628, 649 (1972) (collecting sources) ("[C]ruelty of capital punishment lies not only in the execution itself and the pain incident thereto, but also in the dehumanizing effects of the lengthy imprisonment prior to execution during which the judicial and administrative procedures essential to due process of law are carried out" (footnote omitted)); *District Attorney for Suffolk Dist. v. Watson,* 381 Mass. 648, 673 (1980) (Braucher, J., concurring) (death penalty unconstitutional under State Constitution in part because "[it] will be carried out only after agonizing months and years of uncertainty"); *see also Riley v. Attorney General of Jamaica,* [1983] 1 A.C. 719, 734–735 (P.C. 1982) (Lord Scarman, joined by Lord Brightman, dissenting) ("execution after inordinate delay" would infringe prohibition against "cruel and unusual punishments" in § 10 of the

"Bill of Rights of 1689," the precursor to our Eighth Amendment); *Pratt v. Attorney Gen. of Jamaica,* [1994] 2 A.C. 1, 4 (P.C. 1993); *id.,* at 32–33 (collecting cases finding inordinate delays unconstitutional or the equivalent); *State v. Makwanyane* 1995 (3) SA391 (CC) (S. Afr.); *Catholic Commission for Justice & Peace in Zimbabwe v. Attorney-General,* [1993] 1 Zim. L. R. 242, 282 (inordinate delays unconstitutional); *Soering v. United Kingdom,* 11 Eur. Ct. H. R. (ser. A), p. 439 (1989) (extradition of murder suspect to United States would violate the European Convention on Human Rights in light of risk of delay before execution); *United States v. Burns,* [2001] 1 S.C.R. 283, 353, ¶ 123 (similar).

88. *See Ring v. Arizona,* 536 U.S. 584, 615 (2002) (BREYER, J., concurring in judgment).

89. *See, e.g., Gregg,* 428 U.S., at 183 (joint opinion of Stewart, Powell, and Stevens, JJ.).

90. *Compare ante, Glossip,* 135 S. Ct. at 2748–49 (SCALIA, J., concurring) (collecting studies finding deterrent effect), *with e.g.,* Sorensen, Wrinkle, Brewer, & Marquart, *Capital Punishment and Deterrence: Examining the Effect of Executions on Murder in Texas,* 45 Crime & Delinquency 481 (1999) (no evidence of a deterrent effect); Bonner & Fessenden, Absence of Executions: A Special Report, States with No Death Penalty Share Lower Homicide Rates, N.Y. Times, Sept. 22, 2000, p. A1 (from 1980–2000, homicide rate in death-penalty States was 48% to 101% higher than in non-death-penalty States); Radelet & Akers, *Deterrence and the Death Penalty: The Views of the Experts,* 87 J. Crim. L. & C. 1, 8 (1996) (over 80% of criminologists believe existing research fails to support deterrence justification); Donohue & Wolfers, *Uses and Abuses of Empirical Evidence in the Death Penalty Debate,* 58 Stan. L. Rev. 791, 794 (2005) (evaluating existing statistical evidence and concluding that there is "profound uncertainty" about the existence of a deterrent effect).

91. National Research Council, *Deterrence and the Death Penalty* 2 (D. Nagin & J. Pepper eds. 2012); *accord, Baze v. Rees,* 553 U.S. 35, 79 (2008) (Stevens, J., concurring in judgment) ("Despite 30 years of empirical research in the area, there remains no reliable statistical evidence that capital punishment in fact deters potential offenders").

92. *See Ring, supra,* at 615 (one might believe the studies "inconclusive").

93. DPIC, Execution List 2014, *supra.*

94. BJS 2013 Stats, at 19 (Table 16).

95. *Id.,* at 20 (Table 17); *see also* Baumgartner & Dietrich, Most Death Penalty Sentences Are Overturned: Here's Why That Matters, Washington Post Blog, Monkey Cage, Mar. 17, 2015 (similar).

96. *See Furman,* 408 U.S., at 311–12 (White, J., concurring) (It cannot "be said with confidence that society's need for specific deterrence justifies death for so few when for so many in like circumstances life imprisonment or shorter prison terms are judged sufficient").

97. *But see* A. Sarat, *Mercy on Trial: What It Means To Stop an Execution* 130 (2005) (Illinois Governor George Ryan explained his decision to commute all death sentences on the ground that it was "cruel and unusual" for "family members to go through this . . . legal limbo for [20] years").

98. *Valle v. Florida,* 132 S. Ct. 1, 2 (2011) (Breyer, J., dissenting from denial of stay).

99. *Id.,* at 2.

100. *See* ACLU, *A Living Death: Life Without Parole for Nonviolent Offenses* 11, and n.10 (2013).

101. *See* P. Mackey, *Hanging in the Balance: The Anti–Capital Punishment Movement in New York State, 1776–1861,* p. 17 (1982); T. Jefferson, A Bill for Proportioning Crimes and Punishments (1779), reprinted in *The Complete Jefferson* 90, 95 (S. Padover ed. 1943); 2 *Papers of John Marshall* 207–209 (C. Cullen & H. Johnson, eds. 1977) (describing petition for commutation based in part on 5-month delay); *Pratt v. Attorney Gen. of Jamaica,* [1994] 2 A. C., at 17 (same in United Kingdom) (collecting cases).

102. *Infra,* at 2770–73. [*Ed. note:* This citation, citing pages in the *Supreme Court Reporter,* references a later portion of Justice Breyer's own dissent in *Glossip. See Glossip,* 135 S. Ct. at 2770–73.]

103. *Atkins,* 536 U.S., at 319 (quoting *Enmund v. Florida,* 458 U.S. 782, 798 (1982); internal quotation marks omitted); *see also Gregg,* 428 U.S., at 183 (joint opinion of Stewart, Powell, and Stevens, JJ.) ("sanction imposed cannot be so totally without penological justifica-

tion that it results in the gratuitous infliction of suffering"); *Furman, supra,* at 312 (White, J., concurring) (a "penalty with such negligible returns to the State would be patently excessive and cruel and unusual punishment violative of the Eighth Amendment"); *Thompson,* 556 U.S., at 1115 (statement of Stevens, J., respecting denial of certiorari) (similar).

104. *Furman, supra,* at 431–32 (Powell, J., dissenting); *see also* J. Jeffries, *Justice Lewis F. Powell, Jr.,* p. 409 (2001) (describing Powell, during his time on the Court, as a "fervent partisan" of "the constitutionality of capital punishment").

105. Habeas Corpus Reform, Hearings before the Senate Committee on the Judiciary, 100th Cong., 1st and 2d Sess., 35 (1989 and 1990).

106. Jeffries, *supra,* at 452.

107. *Compare* BJS, L. Greenfeld, *Capital Punishment,* 1990, p. 11 (Table 12) (Sept. 1991) with *supra,* at 18–19. [*Ed. note:* The latter citation is a reference to Justice Breyer's own dissent—in particular, the citation references pages in his slip opinion. *See Glossip,* 135 S. Ct. at 2764–65.]

108. Katz & Eckholm, N.Y. Times, at A1.

109. *Ibid.* [*Ed. note:* North Carolina's Center for Death Penalty Litigation took on Henry Lee McCollum's case and worked with private law firms to get DNA testing of physical evidence in the case. DNA testing of a cigarette butt found near weapons used in the murder excluded McCollum but matched to Roscoe Artis, a man who lived only a block away from the crime scene and who had prior sexual assault convictions. *DNA Evidence Clears Two North Carolina Men,* Innocence Project, Sept. 3, 2014, at www.innocenceproject.org/news-events -exonerations/2014/dna-evidence-clears-two-north-carolina-men.]

110. *McCollum v. North Carolina,* 512 U.S. 1254 (1994).

111. *See also* DPIC Innocence List, *supra* (Nathson Fields, 23 years; Paul House, 23 years; Nicholas Yarris, 21 years; Anthony Graves, 16 years; Damon Thibodeaux, 15 years; Ricky Jackson, Wiley Bridgeman, and Kwame Ajamu, all exonerated for the same crime 39 years after their convictions).

112. *See* Part I, *supra.* [*Ed. note:* This is a reference to an earlier section of Justice Breyer's opinion. *See Glossip,* 135 S. Ct. at 2756–59 (Breyer, J., dissenting).]

113. *Lockett v. Ohio,* 438 U.S. 586. [*Ed. note: Lockett v. Ohio* was decided by the U.S. Supreme Court in 1978.]

114. *Gregg,* 428 U.S. 153.

115. *Powell v. Alabama,* 287 U.S. 45 (1932); *Wiggins v. Smith,* 539 U.S. 510 (2003); *Ake v. Oklahoma,* 470 U.S. 68 (1985).

116. *Ring,* 536 U.S. 584; *see also id.,* at 614 (BREYER, J., concurring in judgment).

117. *Atkins,* 536 U.S. 304.

118. *Baze,* 553 U.S. 35.

119. *Ford v. Wainwright,* 477 U.S. 399 (1986).

120. *See, e.g., O'Neal v. McAninch,* 513 U.S. 432 (1995).

121. *But see ante, Glossip,* 135 S. Ct. at 2748–50 (SCALIA, J., concurring). [*Ed. note:* This citation, citing pages in the *Supreme Court Reporter* instead of the slip opinion in *Glossip,* references a portion of Justice Scalia's concurrence in *Glossip* in which Scalia laments "the proliferation of labyrinthine restrictions on capital punishment, promulgated by this Court under an interpretation of the Eighth Amendment that empowered it to divine 'the evolving standards of decency that mark the progress of a maturing society'—a task for which we are eminently ill suited." *Glossip,* 135 S. Ct. at 2749 (Scalia, J., concurring) (quoting *Trop v. Dulles,* 356 U.S. 86, 101 (1958)).]

122. *See, e.g., Zant v. Stephens,* 462 U.S. 862, 885 (1983) ("[A]lthough not every imperfection in the deliberative process is sufficient, even in a capital case, to set aside a state-court judgment, the severity of the sentence mandates careful scrutiny in the review of any colorable claim of error"); *Kyles v. Whitley,* 514 U.S. 419, 422 (1995) ("[O]ur duty to search for constitutional error with painstaking care is never more exacting than it is in a capital case" (internal quotation marks omitted)); *Thompson,* 556 U.S., at 1116 (statement of Stevens, J.) ("Judicial process takes time, but the error rate in capital cases illustrates its necessity").

123. *See Hinton v. Alabama,* 134 S. Ct. 1081. [*Ed. note: Hinton v. Alabama* was decided by the U.S. Supreme Court in 2014.]

124. *See Knight,* 528 U.S., at 998 (BREYER, J., dissenting from denial of certiorari) (one of the primary causes of the delay is the States' "failure to apply constitutionally sufficient procedures at the time of initial [conviction or] sentencing").

125. *Woodson*, 428 U.S., at 305 (plurality opinion); *Hall*, 134 S. Ct. at 2001; *Roper*, 543 U.S., at 568.

126. *Furman*, 408 U.S., at 312 (White, J., concurring); *Gregg*, *supra*, at 183 (joint opinion of Stewart, Powell, and Stevens, JJ.); *Atkins*, *supra*, at 319.

127. BJS 2013 Stats, at 19 (Table 16).

128. BJS 2013 Stats, at 14, 19 (Tables 11 and 16).

129. *See* Appendix A, *infra* (showing sentences from 1977–2014).

130. BJS 2013 Stats, at 19 (Table 16).

131. DPIC, *The Death Penalty in 2014: Year End Report* 1 (2015).

132. *See* Appendix B, *infra* (showing executions from 1977–2014).

133. BJS, *Data Collection: National Prisoner Statistics Program* (BJS Prisoner Statistics) (available in Clerk of Court's case file).

134. DPIC, *The Death Penalty in 2014, supra*, at 1.

135. *Atkins*, 536 U.S., at 313–16; *Roper, supra*, at 564–66.

136. E. Mandery, *A Wild Justice: The Death and Resurrection of Capital Punishment in America* 145 (2013).

137. *See* DPIC, *States With and Without the Death Penalty*, at www.deathpenalty info.org/states-and-without-death-penalty.

138. DPIC, *Executions by State and Year*, at www.death penalty-info.org/node/5741.

139. BJS Prisoner Statistics (Delaware, Idaho, Indiana, Kentucky, Louisiana, South Dakota, Tennessee, Utah, Washington).

140. *See* DPIC, *Number of Executions by State and Region Since 1976*, at www.deathpenalty info.org/number-executions-state-and-re gion-1976.

141. DPIC, *Executions by State and Year, supra*; DPIC, *Death Sentences in the United States From 1977 by State and by Year*, at www.deathpenaltyinfo.org/death-sentences-united-states-1977-2008.

142. *See* Appendix C, *infra*.

143. *See supra*, *Glossip*, 135 S. Ct. at 2761–62 (Breyer, J., dissenting). [*Ed. note:* This citation, citing pages in the *Supreme Court Reporter* instead of the slip opinion, references an earlier portion of Justice Breyer's own dissent in *Glossip*.]

144. Liebman & Clarke 264–265; *cf. id.*, at 266. (counties with 10% of the Nation's population imposed 43% of its death sentences).

145. *See* Appendix D, *infra* (such counties colored in red) (citing Ford, The Death Penalty's Last Stand, The Atlantic, Apr. 21, 2015).

146. *See* Appendix E, *infra*.

147. Liebman & Clarke 265–266, and n.47; *cf. ibid.* (counties with less than 5% of the Nation's population carried out over half of its executions from 1976–2007).

148. *See Furman*, 408 U.S., at 311 (1972) (White, J., concurring) (executions could be so infrequently carried out that they "would cease to be a credible deterrent or measurably to contribute to any other end of punishment in the criminal justice system . . . when imposition of the penalty reaches a certain degree of infrequency, it would be very doubtful that any existing general need for retribution would be measurably satisfied"). [*Ed. note:* The use of America's death penalty has become rare—and thus more unusual over time—as life-without-parole (LWOP) sentences have become popular. There are now fewer than 3,000 American death row inmates. The number of people serving LWOP sentences in the United States, however, is far higher. As of 2012, 49,081 inmates were serving LWOP sentences in U.S. prisons. John D. Bessler, *The Death Penalty in Decline: From Colonial America to the Present*, 50 Crim. L. Bull. 245, 260 (2014) (citing *Life Goes On: The Historic Rise in Life Sentences in America* (Washington, DC: The Sentencing Project, 2013), p. 1). While LWOP sentences for first-degree murder are now fairly common or *usual*, death sentences—comparatively speaking—have become very uncommon or *unusual*.]

149. *Roper*, 543 U.S., at 566 (quoting *Atkins, supra*, at 315) (finding significant that five States had abandoned the death penalty for juveniles, four legislatively and one judicially, since the Court's decision in *Stanford v. Kentucky*, 492 U.S. 361 (1989)).

150. DPIC, *States With and Without the Death Penalty, supra*. [*Ed. note:* Nebraska lawmakers voted to abolish the death penalty in 2015, overriding the veto of that state's Republican governor, Pete Ricketts. Julie Bosman, Nebraska Bans Death Penalty, Defying a Veto, N.Y. Times, May 27, 2015. A pro-death penalty group gathered enough signatures to postpone—and potentially derail—the repeal, however. A referendum on the state's death penalty will be voted on in November

2016. Paul Hammel, Death Penalty Supporters Put Repeal on Hold till 2016 Vote, Omaha World-Herald, Oct. 16, 2015.]

151. Seelye, Measure to Repeal Death Penalty Fails by a Single Vote in New Hampshire Senate, N.Y. Times, Apr. 17, 2014, p. A12; Dennison, House Deadlocks on Bill to Abolish Death Penalty in Montana, Billings Gazette, Feb. 23, 2015; *see also* Offredo, Delaware Senate Passes Death Penalty Repeal Bill, Delaware News Journal, Apr. 3, 2015.

152. *Supra, Glossip*, 135 S. Ct. at 2773–74 (Breyer, J., dissenting). [*Ed. note:* This citation, citing pages in the *Supreme Court Reporter* instead of the slip opinion in *Glossip*, references an earlier portion of Justice Breyer's own dissent in *Glossip*.]

153. *See* Yardley, Oregon's Governor Says He Will Not Allow Executions, N.Y. Times, Nov. 23, 2011, p. A14 (Oregon); Governor of Colorado, Exec. Order No. D2013-006, May 22, 2013 (Colorado); Lovett, Executions Are Suspended by Governor in Washington, N.Y. Times, Feb. 12, 2014, p. A12 (Washington); Begley, Pennsylvania Stops Using the Death Penalty, Time, Feb. 13, 2015 (Pennsylvania); *see also* Welsh-Huggins, Associated Press, Ohio Executions Rescheduled, Jan. 30, 2015 (Ohio).

154. *See Atkins, supra,* at 315–16; DPIC, *States With and Without the Death Penalty, supra.*

155. DPIC, *Executions by State and Year, supra*; BJS, T. Snell, *Capital Punishment,* 1999, p. 6 (Table 5) (Dec. 2000) (hereinafter BJS 1999 Stats); BJS 2013 Stats, at 19 (Table 16); von Drehle, Bungled Executions, Backlogged Courts, and Three More Reasons the Modern Death Penalty Is a Failed Experiment, Time, June 8, 2015, p. 26. [*Ed. note:* Ultimately, three men were sentenced to death in Texas in 2015. *See* Texas Death Penalty Developments in 2015: The Year in Review, Texas Coalition to Abolish the Death Penalty, Dec. 15, 2015, at www .tcadp.org/2015/12/15/texas/.]

156. BJS 1999 Stats, at 6 (Table 5); BJS 2013 Stats, at 19 (Table 16).

157. Wilson, Support for Death Penalty Still High, But Down, Washington Post, GovBeat, June 5, 2014, at www.washingtonpost .com/blogs/govbeat/wp/2014/06/05/support-for-death-penalty-still -high-but-down; *see also* ALI, *Report of the Council to the Membership on the Matter of the Death Penalty* 4 (Apr. 15, 2009) (withdrawing

Model Penal Code section on capital punishment section from the Code, in part because of doubts that the American Law Institute could "recommend procedures that would" address concerns about the administration of the death penalty); *cf. Gregg*, 428 U.S., at 193–94 (joint opinion of Stewart, Powell, and Stevens, JJ.) (relying in part on Model Penal Code to conclude that a "carefully drafted statute" can satisfy the arbitrariness concerns expressed in *Furman*).

158. Oakford, UN Vote Against Death Penalty Highlights Global Abolitionist Trend—and Leaves the U.S. Stranded, Vice News, Dec. 19, 2014, at https://news.vice.com/article/un-vote-against-death-penalty-highlights-global-abolitionist-trend-and-leaves-the-us-stranded.

159. International Commission Against Death Penalty, *Review 2013*, pp. 2–3.

160. *Id.*, at 3.

161. *Id.*, at 2.

162. Amnesty International, *Death Sentences and Executions 2013*, p. 3 (2014).

163. *Id.*, at 2.

164. *See, e.g.*, Berman, Nebraska Lawmakers Abolish the Death Penalty, Narrowly Overriding Governor's Veto, Washington Post Blog, Post Nation, May 27, 2015 (listing cost as one of the reasons why Nebraska legislators recently repealed the death penalty in that State); *cf. California Commission on the Fair Administration of Justice, Report and Recommendations on the Administration of the Death Penalty in California* 117 (June 30, 2008) (death penalty costs California $137 million per year; a comparable system of life imprisonment without parole would cost $11.5 million per year), at www.ccfaj.org/rr-dp-official.html; Dáte, The High Price of Killing Killers, Palm Beach Post, Jan. 4, 2000, p. 1A (cost of each execution is $23 million above cost of life imprisonment without parole in Florida). [*Ed. note:* A study done in 2011 found that taxpayers spent four billion dollars since 1978 on California's death penalty system. Charles Riley, One California Budget Fix: Abolish Death Row, CNN Money, June 20, 2011, at www.money.cnn.com/2011/06/20/news/economy/california_death_penalty/. California's death penalty has been called "dysfunctional." *Boyer v. Davis*, 2016 WL 1723586 *1 (U.S., May 2, 2016) (Breyer, J., dissenting from denial of cert.).]

165. *See Marbury v. Madison,* 5 U.S. (1 Cranch) 137, 177 (1803); *Hall,* 134 S. Ct., at 2000 ("That exercise of independent judgment is the Court's judicial duty").

166. *Hall,* 134 S. Ct., at 1999 (quoting *Coker v. Georgia,* 433 U.S. 584, 597 (1977) (plurality opinion)); *see also Thompson v. Oklahoma,* 487 U.S. 815, 833, n.40 (1988) (plurality opinion).

INDEX

Index

Index